# Flavors of Italy

# Flavors of Italy

S A R A   V I G N O Z Z I
G A B R I E L L A   G A N U G I

# TUSCANY

TIME
LIFE
BOOKS

TIME-LIFE BOOKS IS A DIVISION OF TIME LIFE INC.

TIME-LIFE BOOKS
President and CEO                      George Artandi

TIME-LIFE CUSTOM PUBLISHING
Vice President and Publisher          Terry Newell
Vice President of Sales and Marketing    Neil Levin
Editor for Special Markets            Anna Burgard
Director of Special Sales              Liz Ziehl

TIME-LIFE is a trademark of Time Warner Inc. U.S.A.
Library of Congress Cataloging-in Publication Data
Vignozzi, Sara.
    Tuscany: culinary traditions from the Tuscan provinces / by Sara
Vignozzi and Gabriella Ganugi; with photography by Marco Lanza.
    p. cm. -- (Flavors of Italy)
    Includes index.
    ISBN 0-7370-0011-2
    1. Cookery, Italian--Tuscan style. 2. Cookery--Italy--Tuscany.
I. Ganugi, Gabriella. II. Title. III. Series.
TX723.2.T86V54 1999
641.5945'5--DC21          98-52937
                   CIP
                     r98

Copyright © McRae Books Srl 1999

This book was conceived, edited and designed by McRae Books Srl, Florence Italy.
Text: Sara Vignozzi, Gabriella Ganugi      Photography: Marco Lanza
Set Design: Rosalba Gioffré               Design: Marco Nardi
Translation from the Italian: Sara Harris     Editing: Anne McRae,
(in association with First Edition)          Mollie Thomson, Alison Leach

Color separations: Fotolito Toscana, Florence, Italy
Printed and bound in Italy by Grafiche Editoriali Padane

Cover photographs: Front cover, Index Stock Photography, Inc.
Back cover, counterclockwise from top left: Marco Lanza, Giuliano Cappelli, Marco Lanza, Giuliano
Cappelli, Giuliano Cappelli, Marco Lanza

Cover design: WorkHorse Creative

# Contents

# Introduction

The origins of Tuscan cooking date back almost 3,000 years to when the region was settled by the Etruscans, a mysterious people who are thought to have migrated to central Italy from Asia Minor. Their tombs contain beautiful frescoes showing, among other things, *pappardelle* (noodles), pasta wheels for cutting pasta, colanders, cheese graters, grilled steaks, and even *Schiacciata con l'Uva* (Black Grape Sweet Bread — see recipe, page 104). Other frescoes show Etruscan diners reclining elegantly, plates and wine goblets in hand being served by graceful young men and women while musicians play nearby.

Etruscan civilization was eclipsed by the growth of Rome to the south and by the 3rd century BC the ancient region of Etruria had been absorbed into the Roman Republic. Something of Roman cookery has come down to us in the form of a cookbook containing five hundred recipes written or collected by Marcus Gavius Apicius in about 30 BC. None of the dishes described have survived, mainly because they relied heavily on spices and flavorings (at least ten in each recipe) and made generous use of a strong fish sauce, known as *garum*, which was smothered over everything in much the same way as some people use ketchup today.

The Roman world was destroyed by Germanic invaders in the 5th century. Florence and the other villages and towns of Tuscany endured their share of invasion and sacking; population declined and people moved away from the cities, back to the country. Many of Tuscany's most typical dishes date to this time. Starving peasants filled up on bread which was made without salt, a precious import that only the wealthy could afford. Tuscan bread is *sciarpo* (saltless) to this day. Servants in the great halls of the feudal lords

*The founding of the city of Florence is traditionally dated to 59 BC, when the Romans established a colony on the northern bank of the Arno, at a place where the river could be forded easily. The Romans in Tuscany, like their counterparts elsewhere, are notorious for their banquets when rare and costly delicacies were served more with the aim of impressing guests than flattering their tastebuds. Menus included absurd dishes, such as the tongues of parrots and flamingoes, and peacocks' brains. Everyday food was more sober, based on cereals, fish, vegetables, and cheese.*

*In central Tuscany the wealth of Siena was based on trading cloth, locally produced saffron, wine, wax, and spices of all kinds. Like Florence, Siena was a republic, governed by powerful guilds rather than feudal lords. One of the best-known late-medieval frescoes was painted in Siena by Ambrogio Lorenzetti in 1337-39. Called* The Effects of Good and Bad Government, *it gives a complete and lively picture of life in the town and country. The detail above shows* Good Government in the Country *with peasants busily plowing, harvesting, fishing, and hunting.*

learned to make nourishing soups and toasts with the scraps of meat- and oil-flavored bread their lords left them. *Ribollita* (see recipe, page 31) and *Crostini Toscani* (see recipe, page 15), are thought to be modern versions of these early medieval dishes.

These difficult centuries passed and by the 12th century the population had grown again, cities were flourishing and trade and exchange of every sort reached far and wide. The larger cities of Tuscany became independent city-states, fighting among themselves for supremacy and control of valuable trade routes. As people grew richer, larger kitchens were installed in houses and cooking generally became more refined. The use of the fork was introduced in Florence during the 14th century, well before many other parts of Italy and Europe. A recipe book from the 14th century by an anonymous Tuscan cook lists fifty-seven recipes, many of which are quite familiar to modern cooks. Dishes include *ravioli, tortelli, maccheroni,* herbal pies, and marzipan.

During the 15th century the Medici family came to the fore in Florence, gradually taking over the government of the city and then the rest of Tuscany. Lorenzo the Magnificent ruled over a splendid court where fine food and drink were considered part of the new Renaissance way of life (see pages 76–77). Although the last of the Medici rulers in the 17th-18th centuries were mainly dreary religious bigots, the cities of Tuscany continued to celebrate traditional non-religious feast days, such as the *Palio* (a horse race through the city streets, still held twice each summer in Siena), flag twirling and throwing contests, archery, jousting, and football. Religious festivals included Christmas, *Carnevale*, Easter, the Virgin Mary's birth date, the date of the Annunciation, and many others. Most of these traditional festivals are still celebrated today. Now, as then, each occasion is marked by its own special array of dishes, and culinary lore and traditions (see pages 90 91).

When the last member of the Medici family died in 1737, Tuscany passed under the control of the Austrian Grand Dukes of Lorraine and, between 1799 and 1814, under the French when Napoleon defeated the Austrians. Local cooking was eclipsed under Napoleon and it was at this time that many French food words entered Italian, such as "menu," "restaurant," "café," "soirée," "dessert," and others.

Foreign rule of Tuscany ended in 1859 and the region became a part of the newly united Kingdom of Italy in 1860. Florence was capital of Italy from 1861 to 1875. The city was greatly damaged by the remodelling it was given for its new, prestigious role. The Old Market in the city center was destroyed, and many of the traditional trattorias and simple eating houses and their centuries-long tradition simply disappeared. Cooking at this time tended to pretentious and over-refined, having lost the dignity of its native heritage.

*Tuscany lived its period of greatest glory during the Renaissance, which was practically invented in the region. This detail of a fresco, by Sodoma, comes from the abbey of Monte Oliveto Maggiore, in the province of Siena.*

*Fresh food and produce markets, as well as seasonal feastivals, are held daily throughout Tuscany.*

Since then Tuscan cooking has returned to its rural, peasant roots. It relies on the use of the finest and freshest of local ingredients prepared with care, but ideally brought to table as close as possible to the way nature herself made them. Uncomplicated dishes are cooked simply and given extra taste by the use of local herbs, such as basil, rosemary, thyme, parsley, and sage. Meat and fish are typically broiled (grilled) or roasted with plenty of oil and herbs, or gently simmered in oil or a vegetable-based sauce until the meat is tender and flavorful. Meat, fish, and vegetables are also deep-fried in the region's excellent olive oil.

Pasta dishes are less common than in other regions. Tuscan first courses are often bread-based preparations, such as *Pappa al Pomodoro* (see recipe, page 32), *Panzanella* (see recipe, page 29) and *Ribollita* (see recipe, page 31), or broth with beans or fava beans (broad beans) and a little pasta (*Pasta e Ceci* – see recipe, page 34).

*Bistecca alla Fiorentina* (see recipe, page 78) is probably the most well-known Tuscan main course. For lovers of red meat it is the ultimate treat. Beef, veal, pork, and lamb are the most common meats, but there are also many dishes based on duck, rabbit, and other game. Fresh fish and seafood is plentiful along the coast and local traditions make the best of this. *Spaghetti allo Scoglio* (see recipe, page 57) and *Cacciucco* (see recipe, page 65) are dishes typical of the coastal provinces. Further inland, freshwater trout are plentiful.

Along with tomatoes, potatoes, squash, and corn, beans were introduced by European explorers returning from America. Tuscan cooks have adopted them all but have reserved a special place in their hearts for beans. *Cannellini, Toscanelli,* and many others are a constant feature on Tuscan menus.

In simple trattorias dessert is often just the choice of a piece of the new season's fruit; other desserts are also simple, usually based on honey, nuts, spices, and other locally grown products and often served with *Vin Santo* (Holy Wine).

*Traditional cheeses are made of ewe's milk and are produced in small, local factories and on farms. Pecorino is the most common cheese, but ricotta is also popular.*

*The quality of Tuscan olive oil makes it ideal for cooking crisp, fried dishes.*

*Tuscan woodlands produce excellent porcini mushrooms as well as black and white truffles.*

*Chestnuts are another typical woodland fruit. As Christmas approaches the streetcorners of Florence are claimed by sellers of* caldarroste *(roast chestnuts).*

Nowadays the restaurants and trattorias in the regional capital of **Florence** offer a broad range of Tuscan cuisine. The city's most typical dishes include *Trippa alla Fiorentina* (see recipe, page 71), *Fegato alla Salvia* (see recipe, page 75), *Fagioli all'Uccelletto* (often served with Italian sausages – see recipe, page 68), *Cenci* (see recipe, page 112), *Zuccotto* (see recipe, page 101), among others. The city's two main markets – San Lorenzo, in the center near the Duomo, and Sant'Ambrogio, near Santa Croce – offer an excellent range of fresh fish, meat, cheese, fruit, and vegetables on a daily basis.

**Massa Carrara**, the northernmost province of Tuscany, is known for excellent fish along the coast, while classic inland dishes include *tortelli*, *testaroli* (whole wheat flat bread served with *pesto* or a mixture of oil, pecorino and parsley), and delicious *minestrone*.

The province of **Lucca** produces some of the best Tuscan olive oil; cooking with animal fats is practically unheard of in Lucca. The area is also known for its bread (the medieval town of Altopascio is particularly famous) and there are many *zuppe* based on cooked bread and vegetables, served with lashings of fresh olive oil. The coastal resort of Viareggio is famous for its fish stew, a spicier version of the one made at Livorno. Inland, the wooded valleys produce black and white truffles and the streams are full of succulent trout.

Southward, along the coast, **Livorno** maintains a genuine tradition of fish cooking, based on the fresh catch caught daily off the coast. Its most famous dish, *Cacciucco* (see recipe, page 65), has been the center of heated debate recently after a multinational firm announced plans to market a packaged, frozen version. The question is yet to be resolved and the directors of the international company have all been invited to Livorno, courtesy of the mayor, to taste the difference. The tiny island of Elba, off the coast, makes its own version of *Cacciucco*, known as *Sburrita*, together with a host of other fresh fish dishes, based on lobster, octopus, and bream, among others.

Nearby **Pisa** has a broad mixture of both fish and inland dishes. Local specialties include *Zuppa di Ranocchi* (Frog Soup) and *Stoccafisso in Agrodolce* (Sweet and Sour Stockfish). The province is also known for its excellent game, including wild boar, duck, pheasant, and venison.

Moving inland in the direction of Florence, the provinces of **Pistoia** and **Prato** produce local sweets, including *Necci*, *Brigidini* (Fennel-Flavored Wafers), and *Castagnaccio* (see recipe, page 107). Prato also produces salami and mortadella, and a wide range of fruit for the Florentine markets.

Southeast of Florence the province of **Arezzo** has a distinctive cuisine. Specialties include *Pappardelle sulla Lepre* (see recipe, page 40), *Scottiglia* (see recipe, page 62), *Crostini all'Aretina* (see recipe, page 23), and *Agnello Arrosto* (Roast Lamb).

**Siena** is known for its cured meats, pecorino cheese, and olive oil. Many Siennese dishes make extensive use of local herbs, such as mint, tarragon, and calamint. A special local pasta, called *Pici* (see recipe, page 45), is worth trying. Siennese prosciutto is particularly tasty.

The southernmost province of **Grosseto** is famous for fish along the coast and game farther inland. Wild boar are plentiful in the Maremma. Local specialties include *Acqua Cotta* (see recipe, page 48), *Polenta alla Maremmana*, and *Risotto di Carciofi*. The pecorino and ricotta cheeses produced in the province are exceptionally good.

*The hilltop town of Montalcino in central Tuscany is famous for its local wines, the best of which – Brunello – is judged as one of Italy's top reds.*

*Fishing is an important industry along the entire coast of Tuscany. In summer tiny fish restaurants sprout up along the beach fronts and serve the day's catch fresh from the nets.*

# Antipasti

Traditionalists will tell you that, with the exception of Chicken Liver Toasts and sliced cured meats, there are no *antipasti* in Tuscan cooking, This was true until a generation ago, but with the move to lighter meals in modern Tuscany, appetizers are often served instead of a pasta dish or second course. And on special occasions ... several *antipasti* will appear on the table, before the pasta dish!

# Crostini Toscani

## *Chicken Liver Toasts*

*Serves 6-8*
*Preparation: 35 minutes*
*Cooking: 30 minutes*
*Recipe grading: fairly easy*

Skin the calf's milt and cut into small pieces. ❧ Trim any connective tissue and discolored parts from the chicken livers and chop into small pieces. ❧ Finely chop the anchovy fillets and capers together. ❧ Melt two-thirds of the butter in a nonstick skillet over a moderate heat. Add the onion and sauté until tender, stirring frequently. ❧ Add the chicken livers and calf's milt, if used, and cook for 5 minutes, stirring frequently. ❧ Season with salt and pepper, add the wine, and cook for 15 minutes, stirring frequently. If the mixture dries out, moisten with a little stock. ❧ Remove the skillet from the heat and set aside to cool a little. ❧ Place the liver mixture on a chopping board and chop finely. ❧ Heat the oil in the skillet over a moderate heat and add the liver mixture, anchovies, and capers. Stir well, add the remaining butter, and cook for 3-4 more minutes. ❧ Spread this deliciously rich, savory mixture on the toasts and keep warm in the oven until just before serving.

- 7 oz/200 g calf's milt (optional, see below)
- 8 oz/250 g chicken livers
- 4 anchovy fillets
- 2 tablespoons/2 oz/60 g capers
- 3 tablespoons /1½ oz/45 g butter
- 1 onion, finely chopped
- salt to taste
- freshly ground black pepper
- ½ cup/4 fl oz/125 ml dry white wine
- ½ cup/4 fl oz/125 ml beef stock (homemade or bouillon cube)
- 4 tablespoons extra-virgin olive oil
- 1 long loaf firm-textured white bread, (about 3 in/7.5 cm in diameter), cut in ½ in/1 cm thick slices and toasted in the oven

*Suggested wine: a young, fruity red (Chianti Montalbano)*

*The traditional recipe calls for milt (calf's spleen). If preferred, omit and double the quantity of chicken livers.*

# Fettunta
## *Toasted Bread with Garlic and Oil*

*Serves 4*

*Preparation: 10 minutes*

*Cooking: 5 minutes*

*Recipe grading: very easy*

- 8 slices firm-textured white bread, ½ in/1 cm thick
- 2 large whole cloves garlic
- salt to taste
- freshly ground black pepper
- 3½ tablespoons best quality extra-virgin olive oil

*Suggested wine: a young, sparkling red (Vino Novello)*

In Tuscany, the new season's oil, just pressed, is used for this simple but delicious snack. Ideally, the bread should be toasted over the glowing embers of a wood fire. Otherwise, toast it in a preheated oven at 400°F/200°C/gas 6, until crisp. It is important that the bread dries out while toasting, which it won't if browned in a toaster. ✎ Rub each slice all over with the garlic. ✎ Arrange the toasted bread on a serving platter. Season with salt and pepper and drizzle with the oil.

To make *bruschetta*, top each slice with about 2 tablespoons of diced and seeded ripe tomatoes and sprinkle with torn fresh basil leaves. ✎ Other Tuscan toppings include lightly boiled, shredded dark cabbage leaves, and home-cooked cannellini beans.

*Try to buy traditionally baked white bread, with a dense, ivory-colored crumb, such as a Tuscan loaf or French pain de campagne, a day or two in advance. Mass-produced steam-baked bread is not suitable.*

# Insalata di Campo

## *Peasant-Style Mixed Salad*

Wash all the salad vegetables very thoroughly in cold running water, drain well and then gently squeeze them dry in a clean cloth. ❧ Place the leaves, whole or coarsely torn, in a large salad bowl. Sprinkle with salt and pepper and drizzle with the vinegar and, lastly, the oil. ❧ Toss vigorously and serve with plenty of fresh crusty bread.

*Serves 6*
*Preparation: 25 minutes*
*Cooking: none*
*Recipe grading: easy*

- 2½ lb/1.2 kg (untrimmed weight) mixed endive/chicory and radicchio varieties (red, pale yellow and white, green and white)
- 7 oz/200 g young, tender, dark green cabbage leaves, (optional)
- salt to taste
- freshly ground black pepper
- red wine vinegar
- extra-virgin olive oil

*The original Tuscan recipe calls for wild chicory, which is gathered by pulling the plant, root and all, from the ground; the slightly bitter roots are considered the best part, with only the outermost layer of skin scraped away with a small, sharp knife. If possible, use several types of radicchio and endive/ chicory, chosen from red varieties such as Treviso, Chioggia, Castelfranco; white or white and green Belgian endive/chicory and escarole/curly endive.*

# Affettati Misti

## *Mixed Platter of Cured Tuscan Meats*

*Serves 4*
*Preparation: 5 minutes*
*Cooking: none*
*Recipe grading: very easy*

Arrange the various meats on a serving platter or dish. ๛ Place the bread in a bread basket and serve with the meats, olives, and pickles.

Given the popularity of Tuscan cooking, all the cured meats listed here can usually be bought from Italian delicatessens or specialty sections of large supermarkets or city food stores. However, if you can't find the exact ones, replace with other, similar types of Italian cured meat.

- 5 oz/150 g Tuscan prosciutto, freshly sliced off the ham
- 4 oz/125 g Tuscan salami
- 4 oz/125 g finocchiona, sliced fairly thickly
- 6 small wild boar sausages
- 1 lb/500 g sliced, firm-textured white bread
- best quality green or black olives
- homemade pickles (optional)

*Suggested wine: a dry red*
*(Chianti Classico)*

*Finocchiona is a large soft salami flavored with fennel seeds. The very best, freshest variety is called Sbriciolona (from the Italian sbriciolare, "to crumble"), because it falls apart as you slice it.*

# Fresh and Cured Meats

All the various provinces of Tuscany produce a variety of cured meats and sausages. Generally speaking, although their names vary from one place to another, they are usually made in the same way. Siena's *buristo* becomes *mallegato* in Lucca and *biroldo* in Pistoia, but the specialty is basically the same. *Buristo* consists of a mixture of pork offcuts, skin, blood, and spices encased in a skin. In Lucca, a handful of tiny sweet raisins and pine nuts are mixed into the blend before it is wrapped and cured.

*Finocchiona* is one of the most distinctive of Tuscan salami; it consists of a mixture of lean and fatty pork with fennel seeds (fennel is called *finocchiona* in Italian, hence the name). The Florentine version — called *Sbriciolona* — is very fresh, soft, and crumbly. It is difficult to slice thinly, so is usually served in rather thick slices. It is commonly served as an appetizer with globe artichokes preserved in oil.

*Selection of cured meats and sausages in a butcher's shop in Florence. The* salamini piccanti *(spicy little salamis) in the foreground are made by adding hot chili peppers to the meat mixture before curing.*

*Tuscan cured raw hams (or* prosciutto crudo*), especially those from Siena, are treated with plenty of salt and pepper, and also often with garlic and juniper berries. This makes them much tastier than hams from Parma or San Daniele. Tuscan ham is often carved into fairly thick slices by hand rather than thinly sliced on a machine. Served on the saltless Tuscan bread and with a glass of good red Chianti, few Tuscans would exchange it for the more famous, sweeter hams from farther north.*

The Maremma, a wild area of reclaimed marhslands in southern Tuscany, is home to many wild animals, including wild boar and deer. Many mouthwatering cured meats and sausages are made from wild boar meat, such as cured raw hams and small, lean sausages which can be sliced like little salami.

In keeping with the peasant tradition that produced so many Tuscan classics, when an animal was butchered every part was used and nothing wasted. Soppressata or soprassata *(the name comes from the Spanish and means "sal presar", or to sprinkle with salt)* is made from various cuts of pig meat, including the animal's skin and jowl. The chopped offcuts are highly seasoned with a mixture of chili pepper, cloves, coriander seeds, and cinnamon. This mixture is then tightly wrapped and sewn up in a linen cloth and simmered for several hours until ready.

*Undoubtedly Tuscany's most famous meat dish,* Bistecca alla Fiorentina *(Florentine Beef Steak – see recipe, page 78) is cut from Chianina beef, a breed native to the Val di Chiana, near Arezzo. The steak is cut from the animal's loin and includes the fillet and T-bone. There is no such thing as a well-done Florentine Beef Steak; it must always be* al sangue *(very rare). It is traditionally accompanied by a side dish of boiled white cannellini beans.* Arista *(roast loin of park) is another Tuscan specialty. Its name comes from the Greek* aristos, *meaning "the best." The loin of pork, with all the chops attached to the backbone, is spiked with garlic and rosemary and slowly roasted in the oven.*

# Crostini con i Funghi

*Mushroom Toasts*

*Serves 4*
*Preparation: 20 minutes*
*Cooking: 25 minutes*
*Recipe grading: easy*

- 1¼ lb/625 g fresh porcini mushrooms
- 1-1½ tablespoons butter
- 4 tablespoons extra-virgin olive oil
- ½ white or Bermuda/mild red onion, finely chopped
- 2 cloves garlic, finely chopped
- 1 tablespoon fresh calamint (or parsley or thyme), finely chopped
- salt to taste
- freshly ground black pepper
- ½ cup/4 fl oz/125 ml vegetable stock (homemade or bouillon cube)
- 1 long loaf firm-textured white bread, (about 3 in/7.5 cm in diameter), cut in ½ in/1 cm thick slices and toasted in the oven

*Suggested wine: a dry white*
  *(Capezzana Bianco)*

Fresh porcini are the most prized wild mushrooms in Tuscany. However, they are often expensive or unobtainable. If you can't get them, experiment with other wild mushrooms, such as shiitake, chanterelles, morels or oyster mushrooms (or combinations of these).

Remove any grit or dirt from the mushrooms, rinse quickly under cold running water, and pat dry with paper towels. ⮞ Separate the stalks from the caps and dice only the firm, unblemished stalks. Chop the caps coarsely. ⮞ Heat the butter and oil in a nonstick skillet over a moderate heat and sauté the onion, garlic, and calamint for 3 minutes. ⮞ Add the mushrooms and season with salt and pepper. Cook for 5 minutes, stirring continuously. ⮞ Gradually stir in enough stock to keep the mixture moist but not sloppy and continue cooking for another 8–10 minutes. ⮞ Spread each toast with a generous helping of the mushroom mixture and serve.

VARIATION: Spread the mushroom mixture on squares of firm, cold polenta and bake in a preheated oven at 400°F/200°C/ gas 6 for 10 minutes before serving.

# Crostini all'Aretina
## *Sausage Toasts*

*Serves 6*
*Preparation: 10 minutes*
*Cooking: 5 minutes*
*Recipe grading: easy*

Squeeze the sausage meat out of the sausage skins into a mixing bowl. ❧ Add the cheese and pepper and mix very thoroughly with a fork. ❧ Spread each toast with a generous helping of the sausage and cheese mixture and transfer to a large, shallow ovenproof dish. ❧ Bake in a preheated oven at 400°F/200°C/gas 6 for 5 minutes, or until the cheese has melted and the topping is bubbling. ❧ Serve piping hot straight from the oven.

- 1³⁄₄ cups/7 oz/200 g small, highly flavored fresh Italian sausages
- 7 oz/225 g fresh stracchino (crescenza) cheese or a coarsely grated semi-hard stracchino cheese,
- freshly ground black pepper
- 1 long loaf firm-textured white bread (about 3 in/7.5 cm in diameter), cut in ½ in/1 cm thick slices and toasted in the oven

*Suggested wine: a young, dry red (Chianti Colli Aretini)*

# Pinzimonio

## *Platter of Raw Vegetables in Olive Oil Dip*

Only the freshest, most tender artichokes are suitable. Have one or two large, juicy lemon wedges ready to rub over all the cut surfaces as you work to prevent discoloration. Remove the tough outer leaves. Cut off the upper section of the remaining leaves, leaving the fleshy, edible base of each leaf attached to the stem. Doing this will expose a central "cone" of leaves: slice about 1 in/2.5 cm off the top of this and part the leaves to gain access to the "choke," the spiny filaments which must be carefully trimmed away, leaving the fleshy, dish-shaped heart intact. Use a small, sharp knife to scrape away the skin from the stalk. As each artichoke is finished, drop it into a bowl of cold water acidulated with the juice of a lemon. Set aside for 15 minutes. ❧ If the carrots are very young and tender, scrub well and leave whole with a little stalk attached. If larger, peel and cut lengthwise into quarters. ❧ Discard the outermost layer of the fennel, cut the bulbs from top to bottom, dividing them into quarters, and rinse well. ❧ Cut the celery heart lengthwise in half or quarters, wash and drain. ❧ Trim and wash the radishes, leaving any fresh, unwilted leaves attached. ❧ Trim the scallions, leaving only a short length of green leaf attached. Unless they are very fresh and firm, remove the outermost layer of the bulb. ❧ Drain the artichokes thoroughly and pat dry with paper towels. ❧ Arrange all the vegetables on a large serving platter. ❧ Place the platter in the middle of the table and give each person a plate and a small bowl. Place containers of oil, vinegar, freshly squeezed lemon juice, salt and pepper on the table and let each diner prepare their own bowl of dressing to dip the vegetables into. ❧ Serve with plenty of fresh bread.

*Serves 6*

*Preparation: 20 minutes + 15 minutes' standing*

*Cooking: none*

*Recipe grading: easy*

- 4–6 very young, fresh globe artichokes
- lemon wedges
- juice of 1 lemon
- 12 very fresh small carrots, preferably with their leaves
- 2 small, tender fennel bulbs
- 1 celery heart
- 12 radishes
- 6 scallions/spring onions
- scant ½ cup/3½ fl oz/100 ml extra-virgin olive oil
- good quality wine vinegar
- scant ½ cup/3½ fl oz/100 ml lemon juice
- salt to taste
- freshly ground black pepper

*Suggested wine: a dry, sparkling white (Spumante di Vernaccia di San Gimignano)*

# Salame e Fichi Freschi

*Tuscan Salami with Fresh Figs*

*Serves 4–6*
*Preparation: 5 minutes*
*Cooking: none*
*Recipe grading: very easy*

- 14 oz/400 g fresh green or black figs
- 10 oz/300 g Tuscan salami, thinly sliced
- 6 fresh fig leaves (optional)

*Suggested wine: a dry rosé (Bolgheri)*

Wash the figs thoroughly under cold running water, then pat dry with paper towels. ঌ Remove the rind from the salami. ঌ If you have them, place the fig leaves on a large serving dish and arrange the salami and figs on top.

*Figs begin to appear in the markets in Florence in June. In August, when the local trees are producing these delicious fruit, this dish becomes a staple in many homes and restaurants. The combination of the salty salami and the sweet flesh of the fruit is a perfect and refreshing way to begin a meal at the end of long, hot summer's day.*

# Cecina

## *Garbanzo Bean Flat Bread*

Place the garbanzo bean flour in a large mixing bowl and using a wooden spoon or a balloon whisk, gradually stir in enough water to form a thick pouring batter with no lumps. ❧ Beat in the oil and a generous dash of salt. ❧ When the batter is smooth, pour into a nonstick roasting pan or ovenproof dish, filling to a depth of less than ¼ in/5 mm. ❧ Bake in a pre-heated oven at 400°F/200°C/gas 6 for 10 minutes. A thin crust should form on the surface. ❧ Transfer the cooked *cecina* to a heated serving dish, sprinkle with freshly ground pepper and serve at once.

*Serves 6*
*Preparation: 5 minutes*
*Cooking: 10 minutes*
*Recipe grading: easy*

- 4½ cups/1¼ lb/625 g garbanzo bean/chick pea flour
- 8¾ cups/3½ pints/2 liters water
- 3/4 cup/6 fl oz/180 ml extra-virgin olive oil
- salt to taste
- freshly ground black pepper

*Suggested wine: a dry rosé (Carmignano)*

*This is just one of the many regional breads made in Italy. Simple and easy to make, it is delicious served hot with a platter of sliced cured meats.*

# Primi piatti

Tuscan first courses are strongly linked to the peasant tradition that created them. Bread was relatively cheap and formed the basis of many meals. Bread-based *primi piatti* are among the most typical Tuscan dishes even today. Soups were common fare, along with homemade pasta, often served with sauces from game typical of the region. Dried, store-bought pasta, such as spaghetti and penne, were not as common in Tuscany as they were farther south, although they are now widely served.

# Panzanella

## *Tuscan Bread Salad*

Slice the bread fairly thickly and soak in water for 3-10 minutes, depending on how firm it is, until it softens but does not disintegrate. ❧ Drain in a colander and squeeze each slice well to remove excess moisture. The bread should resemble large, damp breadcrumbs. ❧ Wash the lettuce leaves, dry thoroughly, and cut into thin strips. ❧ Transfer the bread to a large salad bowl. Add the tomatoes, cucumber, onions, lettuce, and basil and mix gently but thoroughly. ❧ Drizzle with the oil and vinegar and season with salt and pepper. ❧ Chill in the refrigerator for at least 2 hours before serving. ❧ Serve cold.

Serves 4–6

Preparation: 15–20 minutes + 2 hours' chilling

Cooking: none

Recipe grading: easy

- 1¼ lb/625 g firm-textured white bread, about 2 days old
- 8 crisp Romaine/cos lettuce leaves
- 6 medium ripe tomatoes, skinned and cut in quarters or eighths
- 1 large cucumber, peeled and diced
- 2 Bermuda/mild red onions, very thinly sliced
- 10 fresh basil leaves, torn
- 6 tablespoons extra-virgin olive oil
- Italian red wine vinegar
- salt to taste
- freshly ground black pepper

*Suggested wine: a young, dry red (Chianti)*

*The ingredients used to make Panzanella vary according to which part of Tuscany it is made. The addition of cucumber, for example, is shunned in the area around Siena, while it is always included in Florence. The salad can be enriched by adding diced carrots, fennel, celery, hard-cooked eggs, capers, or pecorino cheese.*

# **Ribollita**

## *Vegetable and Bread Soup*

Place the tomatoes in a large, heavy-bottomed saucepan with the beans, garlic, and sage. Cover with cold water. If using fresh beans, add salt to taste at this point. ❧ Bring slowly to a boil, cover and simmer for about 25 minutes for fresh beans or about 1 hour for dried beans. If using dried beans, add salt when they are almost cooked. ❧ Discard the garlic and sage and pureé half the beans in a food processor or food mill. ❧ Put the parsley, thyme, onion, leek, carrots, Swiss chard, cabbage, tomatoes, and other vegetables in a large, heavy-bottomed saucepan with 4 tablespoons of oil over a moderate heat and sauté for a few minutes, stirring continuously. ❧ Add the puréed beans and the whole beans, followed by about two-thirds of the stock. Taste for salt. Cover and simmer gently for about 1½ hours, adding more stock if the soup becomes too thick. ❧ Heat a heavy-bottomed saucepan and add a ladle or two of the soup and a slice of bread. Keep adding more soup and bread until finished. Drizzle with 3 tablespoons of oil and sprinkle with pepper. Cover and leave to stand for 2–3 hours. ❧ Return to the heat and bring slowly to a boil. Simmer very gently for 20 minutes without stirring. Alternatively, reheat the soup in the oven at 425°F/220°C/gas 7 for about 10 minutes. ❧ This soup is equally good served hot, warm or even cold, depending on the season. Traditionally it is served in small, round terra cotta bowls with little handles on either side. Drizzle a little olive oil into the bottom of each, then ladle in the soup.

*Serves 6–8*

*Preparation: 45 minutes + 2–3 hours standing, + 12 hours' soaking, if using dried beans;*

*Cooking: 2–3 hours*

*Recipe grading: fairly easy*

- 3 cherry tomatoes (pricked with a fork)
- 1 lb/500 g fresh white cannellini beans or 1¼ cups/9 oz/275 g dried cannellini (white kidney or great northern) beans, pre-soaked
- 2 cloves garlic
- 6 leaves fresh sage
- 1½ tablespoons finely chopped parsley
- small sprig of fresh thyme
- 1 onion, thinly sliced
- 1 leek, thinly sliced
- 2 medium carrots, diced
- 8 oz/250 g Swiss chard, shredded
- ½ small Savoy cabbage, shredded
- 8 oz/250 g canned Italian tomatoes, coarsely chopped
- a wide variety of seasonal vegetables can also be used, including new potatoes, string/French beans, zucchini/courgettes, peas or whatever you have on hand
- 7 tablespoons extra-virgin olive oil for cooking + extra for serving
- salt to taste
- freshly ground black pepper
- 4¼ cups/1¾ pints/1 liter beef stock
- 10 oz/300 g firm-textured, white or brown bread, sliced about ½ in/1 cm thick

*Suggested wine: a young, dry red (Chianti dei Colli Fiorentini)*

# Pappa al Pomodoro
*Tomato and Bread Soup*

*Serves 4*
*Preparation: 15 minutes*
*Cooking: 25 minutes*
*Recipe grading: easy*

- 1¼ lb/625 g firm, ripe tomatoes
- 5 tablespoons extra-virgin olive oil + extra for serving
- 3 whole cloves garlic, bruised
- 8–10 basil leaves, torn
- 8 oz/250 g firm-textured, white or brown bread, 2 days old, cut in 1¼ in/3 cm thick slices and then diced
- salt to taste
- freshly ground black pepper
- about 1¼ cups/10 fl oz/300 ml water or stock (homemade or bouillon cube)

*Suggested wine: a young, dry red*
*(Chianti dei Colli Senesi)*

Place the tomatoes in a heatproof bowl. Add sufficient boiling water to cover and leave for 1 minute. Drain, rinse quickly in cold water and then skin. Cut in half, remove the seeds and any tough parts, and chop into small pieces. ❧ Heat the oil in a heavy-bottomed saucepan over a low heat, add the garlic and basil, and sauté for 2 minutes before adding the bread. ❧ Increase the heat to moderate and cook, stirring continuously, for 2 minutes. Season with salt and pepper. ❧ Cook for 2 minutes more, then add the tomatoes and a little water or stock. ❧ Continue cooking, uncovered, for 15 minutes, stirring frequently. Add more salt and pepper, if needed, and more liquid if the soup begins sticking to the bottom of the pan, although remember that it is supposed to very thick. ❧ Serve hot in individual soup bowls. Place extra oil and pepper on the table so that each person can season to their own taste.

*A classic peasant dish from the hills around Siena,* Pappa al pomodoro *is excellent when made in advance and reheated. Try adding a few finely chopped fresh rosemary leaves with the tomatoes for extra taste.*

# Pasta e Ceci
## *Pasta and Garbanzo Bean Soup*

*Serves 4*

*Preparation: 20 minutes + 12 hours' soaking*

*Cooking: 1¼ hours*

*Recipe grading: fairly easy*

- 1½ cups/10 oz/300 g dried garbanzo beans/chick peas
- 1 teaspoon baking soda/bicarbonate of soda
- 4 cloves garlic, bruised
- 2 sprigs rosemary
- 6 tablespoons extra-virgin olive oil
- 2 tablespoons tomato purée
- salt to taste
- freshly ground black pepper
- 1–2 cups/8–16 fl oz /250–500 ml stock (homemade or bouillon cube)
- 7 oz/200 g tagliatelle, broken into short lengths

*Suggested wine: a dry red (Pomino)*

*In Tuscany this dish is cooked in a deep, flameproof earthenware dish.*

Put the garbanzo beans in a large bowl of cold water with the soda, and leave to stand overnight or for at least 12 hours. ❧ Drain, transfer to a colander, and rinse thoroughly under cold running water. ❧ Place in a saucepan and cover with cold water. Add 2 garlic cloves and a sprig of rosemary. Cover, leaving a space for steam to escape, and simmer for about 1 hour or until the beans are very tender, adding a pinch of salt after about 50 minutes. ❧ Drain, reserving the cooking water. ❧ Purée three-quarters of the garbanzo beans in a food processor or food mill, keeping the remainder whole. ❧ Heat half the oil in a large heavy-bottomed saucepan and sauté the remaining garlic and rosemary sprig for 3 minutes. ❧ Add the tomato purée and continue cooking over a moderate heat for 2 minutes. ❧ Add the puréed and whole garbanzo beans and the reserved cooking liquid and bring to a boil. If the soup is very thick, dilute with a little hot stock. ❧ Add the tagliatelle and cook for about 10 minutes until the pasta is ready. Season with salt and pepper. ❧ Serve the soup in individual soup bowls. Place extra oil and pepper on the table so that each person can season to taste.

# Gnocchi di Polenta
## *Polenta Gnocchi*

Prepare the meat sauce. ❧ Bring the water to a boil with the salt in a large, heavy-bottomed saucepan. Sprinkle in the cornmeal while stirring continuously with a long-handled wooden spoon to prevent lumps forming. Continue stirring while cooking for 40 minutes. ❧ Just before removing from the heat, stir the butter into the polenta, which should be very thick, smooth and soft in texture. ❧ Using a tablespoon, make oval dumplings, dipping the spoon in cold water to prevent the polenta sticking. Don't worry if the dumplings look rather untidy. ❧ Place a layer of dumplings in a fairly deep, heated ovenproof dish, spoon some meat sauce over the top, and cover with another layer of polenta dumplings. Continue in this way, finishing with a layer of meat sauce. ❧ Sprinkle with the cheese and bake in a preheated oven at 400°F/200°C/gas 6 for 5–8 minutes, or until the topping is golden brown. ❧ Serve immediately.

*Serves 4*

*Preparation: 5 minutes + 15 minutes for the meat sauce*

*Cooking: 50 minutes + 1–2 hours for the meat sauce*

*Recipe grading: fairly easy*

- 8½ cups/3½ pints/2 liters water
- 1 heaped tablespoon coarse sea salt
- 3 cups/1 lb/500 g coarse-grained cornmeal
- ¼ cup/2 oz/60 g butter
- 1 quantity meat sauce (see recipes on pages 45, 50 or 53)
- 1¼ cups/5 oz/150 g freshly grated parmesan cheese

*Suggested wine: a dry red (Chianti Classico)*

*This hearty dish is perfect for cold winter evenings. Prepare in advance and bake just before serving. If pushed for time, use one of the precooked polenta flours which are now widely available.*

# Olive Oil: Tuscany's Liquid Gold

The Tuscan landscape has been dotted with olive trees from Etruscan times, over 2,000 years ago. The fruity, aromatic oil they produce is among the finest in the world. Tuscan farmers harvest and press the slightly immature fruit according to centuries-old tradition. Hand-plucked or shaken from the trees into nets, the olives are pressed within a day of being harvested. The olives are washed, then crushed between large stone wheels into a paste. The oil is extracted from the paste using a centrifuge and then filtered to remove impurities. This *prima spremitura* (first pressing) produces extra-virgin oil, the highest quality available. The oil in the remaining paste is extracted chemically and is of much inferior quality. Extra-virgin Tuscan oil is labor-intensive to produce and expensive to buy (even in Italy), but attempts to save by skimping on quality will ruin every dish. Buy small quantities of new oil and store it in a cool place (not in the refrigerator).

*The beauty of the gnarled, silver-green olive tree has been extolled by poets over the centuries. An evergreen, the olive's tiny white flowers appear in late spring. There are two types of flowers: perfect, with both male and female parts, which develop into fruit; and male, which contain only pollen-producing parts. Trees can live for hundreds of years. The tough, decay-resistant wood is used to make furniture and a variety of utensils.*

Depending on the season, olives are harvested toward the end of November or, according to an old Tuscan proverb, never later than Santa Lucia's day on December 13. To prevent bruising the harvest is still done by hand in most parts of Tuscany. The freshly picked olives are transferred from baskets to colorful canvas sheets and taken straight to the press. The best quality extra-virgin oil is cold-pressed and contains no chemicals or additives of any kind.

Newly pressed oil is a limpid golden green and has an extra, delicious bite in its full, rich flavor. The new season's oil appears in Tuscan shops in December (and in America by January). This is the ideal time to serve Fettunta or Toasted Bread with Garlic and Oil (see recipe, page 16).

Olive oil is graded according to the amount of oleic acid it contains. By Italian law, extra-virgin oil must contain less than 1 percent acidity. Extra-virgin oil is the basic fat used in Tuscan cuisine. Uncooked, it is used to dress salads, to preserve vegetables and fish, and to enliven a wide range of vegetable and antipasta dishes. Heated, it forms the basis of pasta sauces, stews, braised meats, roasts, and many cakes. It is also used for deep-frying.

# Malfatti

## *Spinach Gnocchi*

Bring a large saucepan of salted water to a boil. Add the spinach and cook for 10 minutes. Drain well, squeeze out excess moisture, and chop finely. ❧ Put the spinach in a large mixing bowl and add the ricotta cheese, the egg and extra yolk, half the parmesan, the nutmeg, if using, and salt and pepper. Combine these ingredients very thoroughly with a fork until smooth. ❧ Use a dessertspoon or tablespoon to shape little oval dumplings of the mixture, or roll into small balls between your floured palms, and then press to flatten slightly. Coat lightly with flour all over. ❧ Place the butter and sage leaves in a small saucepan and warm gently to melt the butter. Turn off the heat and leave to stand. ❧ Bring a very large saucepan of salted water to a gentle boil. Add a few drops of olive oil to prevent the dumplings from sticking to one another and then add the dumplings. They should simmer rather than boil. When they bob up to the surface, remove with a slotted spoon. Drain well and place in a heated serving dish. Drizzle with the sage-flavored butter. ❧ Sprinkle with the remaining parmesan cheese and serve at once.

*Serves 4*
*Preparation: 15 minutes*
*Cooking: 20 minutes*
*Recipe grading: fairly easy*

- 1½ lb/750 g trimmed, washed, and drained fresh spinach leaves
- 8 oz/250 g very fresh, drained ricotta
- 1 egg + 1 egg yolk
- scant 1 cup/3½ oz/100 g freshly grated parmesan cheese
- dash of grated nutmeg (optional)
- salt to taste
- freshly ground black pepper
- about 1 cup/4 oz/125 g all-purpose/plain flour
- ¼ cup/2 oz/60 g butter
- 4 fresh sage leaves

*Suggested wine: a young, dry red*
*(Rosso di Montalcino)*

*Malfatti means, literally, "badly made" and refers to the fact that the filling is the same one used for ravioli, but lacks the pasta covering. In some parts of Tuscany these dumplings are also known as* strozzapreti *(priestchokers!)*

# Pappardelle sulla Lepre
## *Ribbon Noodles with Hare*

*Serves 4–6*

*Preparation: 30 minutes + 5–6 hours'
  marinating*

*Cooking: 1¾ hours*

*Recipe grading: fairly easy*

- 1 hare, well hung, cleaned and jointed
- 2 cups/16 fl oz/500 ml full-bodied, dry red wine
- 1 onion, coarsely chopped
- 1 medium carrot, coarsely chopped
- 1 stalk celery, coarsely chopped
- 3 bay leaves
- sprig of rosemary
- large sprig of parsley
- 3 dried juniper berries
- 8 whole black peppercorns
- 1 onion, finely chopped
- 1 stalk celery, finely chopped
- 5 tablespoons extra-virgin olive oil
- about 2 tablespoons/1 oz/ 30 g butter
- 1¼ lb/ 625 g store-bought pappardelle
- scant 1 cup/3½ oz/100g freshly grated parmesan cheese

*Suggested wine: a dry red
(Chianti dei Colli Aretini)*

**The remaining portions of hare
on the bone can be served as
the main course, after this dish.**

Wash the pieces of hare thoroughly and dry with paper towels. Place in a large non-metallic bowl with the wine, the coarsely chopped onion, carrot, and celery, the bay leaves, rosemary, parsley, juniper berries, and peppercorns. Leave for at least 5–6 hours, turning several times. ❧ Remove the hare from the marinade, then strain and reserve the liquid, discarding the vegetables and herbs. ❧ Using a heavy-bottomed saucepan, sauté the finely chopped onion and celery in the oil for 3–4 minutes over a moderate heat. ❧ Add the hare and cook over a slightly higher heat for about 5 minutes, turning the pieces to brown all over. ❧ Ladle some of the reserved marinade over the hare and bring to boiling point. Cover and simmer over a low heat for about 1½ hours, turning the pieces occasionally and adding more marinade as necessary. ❧ Place the cooked hare in a covered dish to keep warm. ❧ Strain the cooking liquid, pressing the vegetables through a sieve (or use a food mill), and add to the liquid to add body. ❧ Select three meaty pieces of hare from the center section or "saddle," remove the meat from the bones, and chop finely. ❧ Melt half the butter in a saucepan and add the cooking liquid and chopped hare. Stir and leave to simmer for 8–10 minutes. ❧ Bring a large saucepan of salted water to a boil, with a few drops of olive oil to prevent the pappardelle sticking to each other. Add the pappardelle and cook for about 8–10 minutes. ❧ Drain well and transfer to a heated serving dish. Stir in the remaining butter, the hare sauce and the parmesan cheese. ❧ Serve immediately.

# Tuscan Bread and Pasta

In the Mediterranean world bread has always been a staple food and Tuscany is no exception to this rule. What is extraordinary about Tuscan bread is that it is totally without salt. Legend has it that this derives from around 1100 when Florence and Pisa were at war. Salt was imported to Florence through the port of Pisa and the Pisans blocked the salt trade in an effort to convince the Florentines to depose arms. Needless to say, the heroic Florentines simply ate their food, and baked their bread, without salt. According to a more prosaic tradition, salt was simply too expensive for most Tuscans and so they baked or bought their bread made from a simple and economical mixture of flour, yeast, and water. Whatever the origin of the custom, traditional Tuscan bread remains saltless to this day. Eaten with flavorful Tuscan toppings, such as chicken liver pâté (see recipe, page 15), and tasty cured meats, the saltless bread provides a striking and satisfying contrast.

*Dante Alighieri, Tuscany's most famous poet and author of The Divine Comedy, was exiled from his beloved Florence by political enemies. During his absence, he mourned his hometown with the phrase "come è salato il pane altrui" (how salty other people's bread is).*

*Bread is the main ingredient in several Tuscan soups and first courses, from a dish called* Panata *(a soup dating back to the 14th century, made of grated two-day-old bread, eggs, cheese, and nutmeg), to* Ribollita *(Vegetable and Bread Soup – see recipe, page 31),* Pappa al Pomodoro *(Tomato Bread Soup – see recipe, page 32), and* Panzanella *(Tuscan Bread Salad – see recipe, page 29). It is also used in a wide range of appetizers, including the many crostini recipes (see pages 15, 22, 23) and a basket of bread is always served with the main course. After dinner, you will see Tuscans sipping the last of the red wine and munching on the last slice of bread.*

Although pasta is less typical of Tuscany than many other regions of Italy, a number of specialties are linked to the region. Over 2,000 years ago the early inhabitants of Tuscany, the Etruscans, prepared large flat noodles with Saracen wheat and water (these are the ancestors of modern lasagna and pappardelle). Nowadays they are generally served with meat or game sauces (Pappardelle sulla Lepre – see recipe, page 40). During the 14th century we know that lasagna was prepared to celebrate San Lorenzo on August 10 when it was offered free to passersby (a tradition that is still observed). Other pasta dishes that have become linked to Tuscany, include Penne Strascicate (see recipe, page 50), Tortelli di Patate (see recipe, page 44) from the Mugello area just north of Florence, and Pici or unsalted homemade pasta (see recipe, page 45), from the Mount Amiata region in central Tuscany.

Spaghetti and penne with tomato or meat sauces are basic fare in any Tuscan restaurant or trattoria. Although they did not originate in Tuscany, tortellini served in meat broth or with meat or tomato sauce are another basic dish that you will find almost everywhere.

Besides the regular Tuscan loaf, there is another type of flat bread which does contain salt and which is brushed with olive oil. Similar to the better-known Focaccia, in Tuscany it is known as Schiacciata all'Olio. Other special breads include a Siennese loaf baked on All Saints Day which has raisins and nuts added to the basic dough. Pan di Ramerino (Rosemary Bread Rolls – see recipe, page 106) are traditionally baked at Easter, while Schiacciata con l'Uva (Black Grape Sweet Bread – see recipe page 104) is made in the fall when the new seasons' grapes ripen on the vines.

# Tortelli di Patate
## *Potato Tortelli*

*Serves 4*

*Preparation: 40 minutes*

*Cooking: about 10 minutes + 30
minutes for boiling the potatoes*

*Recipe grading: fairly easy*

To make the pasta:
- 4½ cups/1 lb/500 g durum wheat flour + ¾ cup/3½ oz/100 g extra flour
- 4 large fresh eggs
- ½ cup/4 fl oz/125 ml milk
- salt

For the filling:
- 1½ lb/750 g floury potatoes, peeled
- 1 large fresh egg
- scant 1 cup/3½ oz/100 g freshly grated parmesan cheese
- 6 tablespoons/3 oz/90 g butter
- freshly grated nutmeg
- salt to taste
- freshly ground black pepper

*Suggested wine: a dry white
(Pomino Il Benefizio)*

Prepare the pasta as explained on page 47. ও Boil the potatoes and when they are cooked but still firm, drain thoroughly and put through a potato ricer or sieve into a large mixing bowl. ও Stir in the egg, a good half of the parmesan cheese, a third of the butter, nutmeg, and salt and set aside. ও Cut the ball of pasta dough in half. Dust the work surface with flour and roll out into two sheets about ⅛–1/16 in/3–1 mm thick. ও. Put teaspoonfuls of the potato mixture onto one sheet at regular intervals, about 1¼ in/3 cm apart, as if making ravioli. ও Place the other pasta sheet on top and run a finger gently between the mounds, then cut between them, sealing the edges of the tortelli with the prongs of a fork. ও Set aside in a single layer on a lightly floured cloth. ও Melt the remaining butter in a small saucepan. ও Bring a large saucepan of salted water to a boil, adding a few drops of oil to prevent the tortelli sticking to one another. Add the tortelli and cook for about 3–4 minutes. ও Remove them as they rise to the surface, using a slotted spoon. ও Transfer to a heated serving dish and drizzle with the melted butter, pepper and the remaining parmesan. ও Serve hot.

*Tortelli di patate are also very good when served with tomato or meat sauce.*

# Pici al Ragù
## *Fresh* Pici *Pasta with Meat Sauce*

*Serves 4*
*Preparation: 50 minutes*
*Cooking: about 1 hour for the meat sauce*
   *+ about 5 minutes for the pasta*
*Recipe grading: fairly easy*

Sift the flour and salt into a large mixing bowl and make a well in the center. Gradually add just enough of the water to make a very firm dough, working it in by hand until the dough is as smooth and elastic. ❧ On a floured work surface, roll the dough out to about ¾ in/2 cm thick and cut into strips. ❧ Roll each strip between your floured palms, slowly drawing it out until it is very thin and resembles rather untidy spaghetti. ❧ Spread the *pici* out on a lightly floured clean cloth. ❧ Sauté the onion, carrot, celery, and parsley in the oil in a heavy-bottomed saucepan for 5 minutes. ❧ Add the beef and sausage meat, squashing any lumps that may form. Stir while cooking for 5 minutes before adding the mushrooms. ❧ Add the wine and cook over a higher heat, uncovered, for 5 minutes to reduce. ❧ Add the tomatoes and salt and pepper to taste. ❧ Reduce the heat, cover and simmer for at least 45 minutes, adding a little stock to moisten. ❧ Bring a large saucepan of salted water to a boil, add the *pici* and cook until tender. ❧ Drain well and transfer to a heated serving dish, add the meat sauce, and toss gently. ❧ Sprinkle with the cheese and serve hot.

To make the pasta:
- 2½ cups/10 oz/300 g durum wheat flour
- dash of salt
- 1 cup/8 fl oz/250 ml hot water

For the sauce:
- 1 medium onion, finely chopped
- 1 medium carrot, finely chopped
- 1 small stalk celery, finely chopped
- 1½ tablespoons finely chopped parsley
- 6 tablespoons extra-virgin olive oil
- 2½ cups/10 oz/300 g ground lean beef
- 1 fresh Italian pork sausage, skinned
- 1 cup/1 oz/25 g dried porcini mushrooms, soaked for 20 minutes in warm water, well drained and coarsely chopped
- ½ cup/4 fl oz/125 ml dry red wine
- 2 cups/14 oz/400 g chopped canned Italian tomatoes
- 1 cup/8 fl oz/250 ml meat stock (homemade or bouillon cube)
- salt to taste
- freshly ground black pepper
- scant 1 cup/3½ oz/100 g freshly grated parmesan cheese

*Suggested wine: a dry red*
*(Rosso di Montalcino)*

# Minestrone Livornese
## *Livorno-Style Minestrone*

*Serves 6*
*Preparation: 35 minutes*
*Cooking: about 3½ hours*
*Recipe grading: fairly easy*

- 1½ cups/10 oz/300 g rice (Italian semifino, cristallo or Carolina rice)
- 1 lb/500 g freshly hulled/shelled borlotti or similar beans or 1¼ cups/8 oz/250 g dried borlotti beans, pre-soaked
- 10 oz/300 g spinach leaves
- 4 oz/125 g leaves of Swiss chard, stalks removed
- ½ small Savoy cabbage
- ¼ cup/2 oz/60 g finely chopped pancetta
- 2 cloves garlic, finely chopped
- 1½ tablespoons finely chopped parsley
- 1½ tablespoons finely chopped fresh basil
- 6 tablespoons extra-virgin olive oil
- 1 onion, coarsely chopped
- 1 medium carrot, coarsely chopped
- 2 stalks celery, coarsely chopped
- 2 zucchini/courgettes, coarsely chopped
- 2 yellow potatoes, coarsely chopped
- salt to taste
- freshly ground black pepper
- 8½ cups/3½ pints/2 liters meat stock (homemade or bouillon cube)
- scant 1 cup/3½ oz/100 g freshly grated parmesan cheese

*Suggested wine: a dry red*
*(Chianti dei Colli Pisani)*

Cover the beans with salted water and boil for about 15 minutes until tender. If using pre-soaked dried beans, drain, rinse and boil until tender, adding salt when they are nearly done. ❧ Wash all the green leaf vegetables well. Shred or cut into thin strips. ❧ Place first the cabbage, then the chard and spinach in a saucepan containing a little salted water and cook for 5–6 minutes. Drain when only just tender, squeeze out excess moisture and chop finely. ❧ Sauté the pancetta, garlic, parsley, and basil in the oil for 4–5 minutes. ❧ Add the raw vegetables followed by the beans and their cooking liquid, then the cooked, chopped vegetables, stirring to combine. ❧ Pour in the hot stock, season to taste, cover and simmer very gently for 2½ hours. ❧ Add the rice, stir well and cook for 20 minutes more. ❧ Serve hot and with extra grated parmesan cheese to sprinkle over the top.

# Ravioli del Casentino

*Casentino Ravioli*

Heap the flour up into a mound on a marble pastry slab or wooden board or work surface. Make a well in the center and break the eggs into it with a generous dash of salt. Using your hand (fingers together) as a "paddle", or a fork, stir the eggs and gradually incorporate the flour, working with your hands once most of the flour has been absorbed. ❧ Knead the dough, sprinkling it with extra flour to prevent it from sticking, until it is smooth and elastic. ❧ Shape into a ball and divide in half or in quarters. Cover with a cloth and set aside. ❧ Place the spinach in a large saucepan of boiling salted water and cook for 8–10 minutes. Drain, squeeze out excess moisture and chop finely. ❧ In a large mixing bowl, combine the spinach with the ricotta, the eggs and the extra yolk, nutmeg, salt and pepper. ❧ On a floured work surface, roll out each piece of dough until about ⅛–1/16 in/3–1 mm thick. ❧ Cut the pasta sheets into 3 in/7.5 cm squares. Place 2 teaspoons of filling in the center of each and then gather the edges together over it, pinching them firmly. ❧ Place in a single layer on a floured cloth and leave to stand for 2–3 hours. ❧ Bring a large saucepan of salted water to a boil with a few drops of oil to stop the ravioli sticking together. Add the ravioli and cook until they rise to the surface. Remove with a slotted spoon and transfer to a heated serving dish.

*Serves 4*

*Preparation: 30 minutes + 2–3 hours' standing*

*Cooking: 1½ hours*

*Recipe grading: fairly easy*

To make the pasta:
- 3½ cups/14 oz/400 g durum wheat flour or all-purpose/plain flour
- 3 large fresh eggs
- salt to taste

For the filling:
- 2¼ lb/1 kg spinach leaves, washed
- 2¼ cups/1 lb/500 g fresh ricotta, drained
- 2 whole eggs + 1 extra yolk
- 1¼ cups/5 oz/150 g grated parmesan cheese
- dash of grated nutmeg
- salt to taste
- freshly ground black pepper

*Suggested wine: a dry red (Chianti Rufina)*

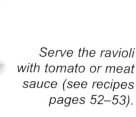

*Serve the ravioli with tomato or meat sauce (see recipes pages 52–53).*

# Acqua Cotta
## *Maremma-Style Soup*

*Serves 4*
*Preparation: 30 minutes*
*Cooking: about 1 hour*
*Recipe grading: fairly easy*

- 5 tablespoons extra-virgin olive oil
- 2 onions, thinly sliced
- 2 cups/10 oz/300 g fresh or frozen peas
- 1¼ cups/7 oz/200 g freshly hulled fava beans/broad beans
- 1 medium carrot, sliced
- 1 stalk celery, thinly sliced
- 1 crumbled dried chili pepper
- salt to taste
- 12 oz/300 g trimmed young Swiss chard or spinach leaves, washed and shredded
- 10 oz/300 g firm, ripe tomatoes, skinned and chopped or 1 cup/8 oz/250 g canned Italian tomatoes, chopped
- 6½ cups/2½ pints/1.5 liters boiling water
- 4 large fresh eggs
- freshly ground black pepper
- ½ cup/2 oz/60 g freshly grated parmesan or pecorino cheese
- 4 slices firm-textured white bread, 2 days old
- 1 clove garlic

*Suggested wine: a dry white*
*(Montecarlo Bianco)*

Pour the oil into a large, heavy-bottomed saucepan. Add the onions, peas, fava beans, carrot, celery, chili pepper, and a dash of salt. ঽ Sauté for about 10 minutes until tender and lightly browned. ঽ Add the chard or spinach and the tomatoes and simmer for 15 minutes. ঽ Pour in the boiling water and leave to simmer gently for 40 minutes, adding more salt if necessary. ঽ Using a fork or balloon whisk, beat the eggs with salt, pepper, and the grated parmesan. ঽ Toast the bread and when golden brown, rub both sides of each slice with the garlic. ঽ Place a slice in each soup bowl or in individual straight-sided earthenware dishes, and pour a quarter of the beaten egg mixture over each serving. Give the soup a final stir and then ladle into the bowls. ঽ Serve immediately.

*The Italian name of this sustaining soup, once a peasant dish, means "cooked water".*

# Penne Strascicate
*Florentine-Style Penne*

Serves 4
Preparation: 25 minutes
Cooking: 1¼ hours
Recipe grading: fairly easy

- 1 medium onion, finely chopped
- 1 small carrot, finely chopped
- 1 small stalk celery, finely chopped
- 1½ tablespoons finely chopped parsley
- 6 tablespoons extra-virgin olive oil
- 2½ cups/10 oz/300 g ground lean beef
- ½ cup/4 fl oz/125 ml full-bodied, dry red wine
- 2 cups/14 oz/400 g canned Italian tomatoes, coarsely chopped
- salt to taste
- freshly ground black pepper
- 1 cup/8 fl oz/250 ml meat stock (homemade or bouillon cube)
- 14 oz/400 g penne pasta
- 1 cup/5 oz/150 g freshly grated parmesan cheese

*Suggested wine: a young, dry red (Chianti dei Colli Fiorentini)*

*This hearty dish revives body and soul on cold winter evenings. It is also an excellent way of using up yesterday's leftover pasta.*

Using a deep nonstick skillet, sauté the onion, carrot, celery, and parsley together for 4–5 minutes in the oil. ❧ Add the meat, breaking up any lumps that may form as it cooks. ❧ Once it has browned, pour in the wine and stir for 4–5 minutes. ❧ Add the tomatoes, salt and pepper. Stir well and simmer for another 4–5 minutes. ❧ Add 2–3 tablespoons of the stock, cover and simmer for 40 minutes or longer, stirring in a little more stock at intervals to keep the sauce moist (but not sloppy). ❧ Bring a large saucepan of salted water to a boil and add the pasta. ❧ Cook until just *al dente* but still with plenty of "bite". ❧ Keep the meat sauce warm over a low heat. Add the drained pasta, toss together, and stir for 2–3 minutes so that the pasta is coated thoroughly with the rich sauce and has absorbed its flavors. ❧ Turn off the heat, stir in the parmesan, and serve at once.

# Basic Sauces and Meat Stock

Tuscan cooking boasts a wide variety of basic sauces to serve with pasta, vegetables, fish, and meat. Like all Tuscan cooking, they tend to be simple and sober and to rely more on the freshness and quality of the ingredients used, rather than complicated preparation. Here we have gathered four sauces that lie at the very heart of Tuscan cooking. Master these simple sauces and they will serve you well in a wide range of dishes.

## BASIC TOMATO SAUCE

For four, to serve with pasta, rice, or meat

2 cloves garlic, finely chopped

1 medium carrot, finely chopped

1 medium onion, finely chopped

1 stalk celery, finely chopped

2 tablespoons finely chopped parsley

4 tablespoons extra-virgin olive oil

2 cups/1 lb/500 g fresh or canned tomatoes, skinned and coarsely chopped

salt to taste and freshly ground black pepper

6 fresh basil leaves, torn

Sauté the garlic, carrot, onion, celery, and parsley in the oil for 4–5 minutes. ❧ Add the tomatoes, season with salt and pepper, and simmer, uncovered, over a low heat for at least 45 minutes, or until the sauce has reduced to the required density. ❧ Turn off the heat, stir in the basil, and serve. ❧ For a spicy sauce, add chili peppers to taste. ❧ In late summer, when tomatoes are cheap and plentiful, make a big quantity in a very large, heavy-bottomed pan. Preserve in sterilized glass jars for use throughout the winter. When making large quantities of the sauce, simmer for at least 1½ hours.

## BÉCHAMEL

Although this sauce is strongly identified with French cooking, its origins are Florentine. It is another of the many recipes that left the Tuscan capital's brilliant Renaissance court with Catherine de' Medici when she went north to marry the future King of France.

¼ cup/2 oz/60 g butter

½ cup/2 oz/60 g all-purpose/plain flour

2 cups/16 fl oz/500 ml boiling milk

freshly grated nutmeg

salt to taste

Melt the butter in a small heavy-bottomed pan over low heat. Stir in the flour and cook, stirring continuously, for 1–2 minutes. ❧ Pour in a little of the milk and stir well. Gradually add all the milk, stirring continuously so that no lumps form. Cook over a low heat, stirring all the time, for about 5 minutes. ❧ Season with nutmeg and salt to taste. ❧ Béchamel sauce is used in many baked pasta and vegetable dishes. Use a quantity of Béchamel sauce to revive yesterday's leftover pasta, by stirring it into the pasta and then baking it all in a hot oven for 15 minutes.

**RICH MEAT SAUCE**

For eight, to serve with pasta, rice, or vegetable dishes

2 cloves garlic, finely chopped
1 medium carrot, finely chopped
1 medium onion, finely chopped
1 stalk celery, finely chopped
2 tablespoons finely chopped parsley
1/4 cup/2 oz/60 g coarsely chopped pancetta
4 tablespoons extra-virgin olive oil
2 cups/8 oz/250 g ground veal or beef
1 cup/4 oz/125 g coarsely chopped chicken breast
1 cup/4 oz/125 g finely chopped chicken livers
1 oz/30 g dried porcini mushrooms, soaked in warm water for 20 minutes, then finely chopped
1/2 cup/4 fl oz/125 ml dry red wine
1 lb/500 g fresh or canned tomatoes, skinned and coarsely chopped
salt to taste and freshly ground black pepper

In a large heavy-bottomed saucepan, sauté the garlic, carrot, onion, celery, parsley, and pancetta in the oil over medium heat until the onion turns light gold. ☙ Add the veal or beef, chicken breast, and livers and cook for 5–7 minutes, stirring all the time. ☙ Add the mushrooms and cook for 5 minutes more. ☙ Pour in the wine and cook until it has evaporated. ☙ Add the tomatoes, season with salt and pepper, partially cover and simmer over low heat for at least 2 hours. The longer the sauce cooks, the tastier it will be, so don't be afraid of simmering for 3 or even 4 hours. Add a little hot stock or water if it becomes too dry.

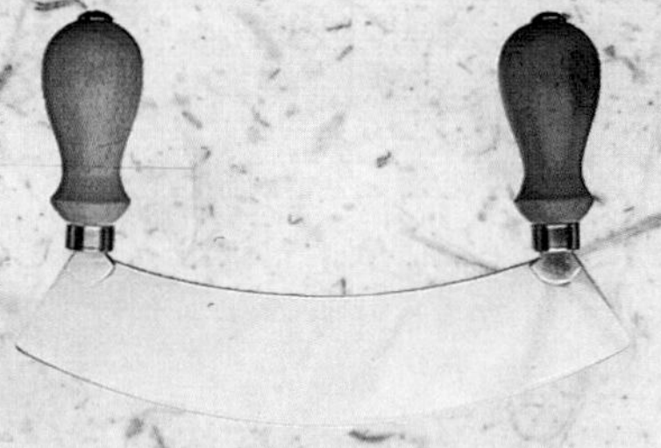

**MEAT STOCK**

Many of the recipes in this book call for a meat stock. You may use stock made with bouillon cube, although the results will be superior if you use homemade stock. Stock freezes very well, so make a large quantity, pour it into small containers (ice-cube trays are ideal) so that it can be used as required. Makes about 6 cups/2 1/2 pints/1.5 liters.

2 1/2 lb/1.2 kg various cuts beef with bones (neck, shoulder, short ribs, brisket)
2 carrots
2 onions
1 large stalk celery
2 ripe tomatoes
2 cloves garlic
2 sprigs parsley
1 bay leaf
8 1/2 cups/3 1/2 pints/2 liters cold water

Put the meat, vegetables, and herbs into a large pot with the water. Cover and bring to the boil over medium heat. Season with salt and pepper. ☙ Partially cover, and simmer over low heat for 3 hours. ☙ Remove from heat and set aside to cool. ☙ When the stock is cool, remove the vegetables and herbs and skim off and discard the fat that will have formed on top.

# Minestra di Farro

## *Spelt and Vegetable Soup*

If using dried beans, soak them overnight in cold water, drain and rinse. Soak the spelt in cold water for at least 4 hours. Cover the beans with cold water and add the garlic, sage, tomatoes (skins pierced with a fork), and a little salt (unless using dried beans). Cover and bring to a boil. Simmer for about 25 minutes, or until tender (longer if dried beans are used, adding salt at the end). Remove and discard the garlic and sage. Purée half the beans in a food mill, reserving the cooking liquid. Heat the oil in a heavy-bottomed saucepan over a moderate heat and sauté the pancetta for 3 minutes with the garlic. Discard the cloves as soon as they start to color. Add the remaining vegetables and the tomato purée, salt, pepper, and stock. Stir well, cover and leave to simmer over a low to moderate heat for 30 minutes before adding the drained spelt. After another 20 minutes, add the two bean mixtures. Adjust the seasoning and simmer for a final 20 minutes. Drizzle each portion with 1 tablespoon of oil and serve hot.

*Serves 4*

*Preparation: 30 minutes + 4 hours' soaking*

*Cooking: about 30 minutes for fresh beans, longer if dried + 1¼ hours*

*Recipe grading: fairly easy*

- 2 cups/14 oz/400 g freshly hulled/shelled cannellini beans or 1 cup/7 oz/200 g dried cannellini beans
- generous 1 cup/7 oz/200 g spelt
- 2 cloves garlic, whole
- small sprig of sage
- 3 cherry tomatoes or small tomatoes
- 6 tablespoons extra-virgin olive oil + extra for serving with the soup
- 3½ oz/100 g finely chopped pancetta
- 2 cloves garlic, lightly bruised
- 1 onion, very thinly sliced
- 1 leek, thinly sliced
- 1 stalk celery, thinly sliced
- 1 carrot, peeled and diced
- 5 oz/150 g young spinach or Swiss chard leaves, washed and shredded
- ½ small, dark green cabbage, washed and shredded
- 3 tablespoons tomato purée
- 6 cups/2½ pints/1.5 liters stock (homemade or bouillon cube)
- salt to taste
- freshly ground black pepper

*Suggested wine: a dry red (Chianti Rufina)*

*Spelt is a cereal grain which has been grown in the Mediterranean since the dawn of farming. It is now available from good wholefood stores. Use pearl barley if you cannot find spelt.*

# Spaghetti allo Scoglio
## *Seafood Spaghetti*

*Serves 4*
*Preparation: 40 minutes + 1 hours'*
*   soaking*
*Cooking: 1 hour*
*Recipe grading: fairly easy*

Soak the mussels and clams for at least an hour to purge them of sand. ❧ Pull the beards off the mussels. Scrub the mussels and clams thoroughly under cold running water. ❧ In a large skillet, sauté 1 clove garlic in 2 tablespoons oil over a moderate heat. Add the mussels and clams with half the wine, cover tightly and cook for 8–10 minutes or until they are open, shaking the pan now and then. ❧ Discard any shells which do not open. Put aside a few of the best ones for garnishing and detach the rest from their shells. ❧ Slice the body sacs of the squid and cuttlefish into rings and strips. ❧ Heat the remaining oil in a large nonstick skillet and sauté the chopped garlic, parsley, and chili peppers for 3–4 minutes. ❧ Add the squid and cuttlefish, season with salt and pepper and stir for 2–3 minutes. Pour in the remaining wine, cover and cook for 12 minutes. ❧ Add the shrimp tails and a little more salt if needed and cook for another 3 minutes before adding the clams and mussels. ❧ Simmer for a final 3 minutes, then turn off the heat. ❧ While the sauce is cooking, bring a large saucepan of salted water to a boil, add the spaghetti and cook until it is tender but still *al dente*. Drain well and combine with the hot seafood sauce. Stir over a low heat for about 2 minutes. ❧ Serve immediately, garnished with the reserved clams and mussels in their shells.

- 1 quart/1 lb/500 g mussels
- 2 dozen (about 1 lb/500 g) very small littleneck clams
- 1 clove garlic
- 8 tablespoons extra-virgin olive oil
- 1 cup/8 fl oz/250 ml dry white wine
- 14 oz/400 g prepared squid
- 14 oz/400 g prepared cuttlefish (or substitute more squid)
- about 10 oz/300 g Pacific shrimp tails/large Mediterranean prawn tails, washed
- 3 cloves garlic, finely chopped
- 2–3 tablespoons finely chopped parsley
- 2 crumbled dried chili peppers
- salt to taste
- freshly ground black pepper
- 12 oz/350 g spaghetti

*Suggested wine: a dry, spicy white (Alicante)*

# Secondi piatti

Almost all main courses are based on meat or fish. Some of the tastiest dishes make use of variety meats, such as tripe or liver. Along the coast, fish and seafood are the most common fare. *Cacciucco*, or Mixed Fish Stew from Livorno, must be the richest of all the fish-based dishes in Tuscany. Farther inland, chicken, beef, and lamb are cooked simply by roasting, grilling, or braising with olive oil and a handful of local herbs. The recipe for Duck with Orange, dating from the Renaissance, recalls Tuscany's days of glory.

# Peposo

## *Spicy Braised Veal*

*Serves 6*
*Preparation: 20 minutes*
*Cooking: 2¹⁄₂ hours*
*Recipe grading: fairly easy*

Pour the oil into a heavy-bottomed saucepan (traditionally a flameproof earthenware casserole dish is used) and sauté the onion, garlic, carrot, celery, and chili peppers for 5 minutes. ❧ Trim any gristle or fat from the meat and cut into 1 in/2.5 cm cubes. ❧ Coarsely crush the peppercorns using a mortar and pestle or place them in a strong paper bag and crush with a rolling pin. ❧ Add the whole garlic and the meat to the saucepan. Season with salt, add the peppercorns, and cook for about 8 minutes, or until the meat is browned all over. ❧ Add the tomatoes, stir well, and cook for 12 minutes. ❧ Pour in the wine. Lower the heat, cover and simmer for 2 hours, stirring occasionally, until the meat is very tender. ❧ Serve very hot.

- 5 tablespoons extra-virgin olive oil
- 1 onion, finely chopped
- 3 cloves garlic, finely chopped
- 2 small carrots, finely chopped
- 2 small stalks celery, finely chopped
- 2 crumbled dried chili peppers
- 2³⁄₄/1.3 kg cubed meat from veal hind shanks/hind shin of veal
- 5 teaspoons whole black peppercorns
- 5 cloves garlic, whole
- salt to taste
- 2½ cups/1¼ lb/625 g chopped canned Italian tomatoes
- 1³⁄₄ cups/14 fl oz/400 ml full-bodied, dry red wine

*Suggested wine: a dry red (Chianti Classico)*

# Paparo all'Arancia
## *Duck with Orange*

*Serves 4*
*Preparation: 25 minutes*
*Cooking: 1½ hours*
*Recipe grading: fairly easy*

- 1 oven-ready duck, weighing 2½ lb/1.2 kg
- 2 cloves garlic, whole
- sprig of rosemary
- salt to taste
- freshly ground black pepper
- 3 oranges (organic: not treated with any fungicide)
- 5 tablespoons extra-virgin olive oil
- 1 onion, coarsely chopped
- 1 carrot, coarsely chopped
- 1 stalk celery, coarsely chopped
- ½ cup/4 fl oz/125 ml dry white wine
- scant ½ cup/3½ oz/100 g superfine or granulated sugar/caster sugar
- 1½ tablespoons water
- 1 tablespoon lemon juice

*Suggested wine: a dry red*
*(Vino Nobile di Montepulciano)*

*Despite French claims to this recipe, it actually originated in the Florentine court of the Medici family during the Renaissance. When Catherine de' Medici went to France to marry the future King Henry II, in the 16th century, she took this and many other secrets of Tuscan cooking with her.*

Wash and dry the duck and put the garlic, rosemary, salt, pepper, and the zest of 1 orange into the cavity. ❧ Pour half the oil into a large roasting pan. Add the duck and sprinkle with more pepper. Arrange the onion, carrot, and celery around the duck and drizzle with the remaining oil. Roast in a preheated oven at 375°F/190°C/gas 5 for about 1½ hours. ❧ Ten minutes into the roasting time, pour the wine over the duck. ❧ Meanwhile, peel the zest off the remaining 2 oranges and cut it into very thin strips. Place in a small saucepan with cold water, bring to a boil and drain. Repeat the process twice to remove bitterness. ❧ In a small, nonstick saucepan heat the sugar, water, and lemon juice over a moderate heat until the sugar melts and caramelizes to a pale golden brown. Add the zest strips, stir over a low heat for 2 minutes and set aside. ❧ Thirty minutes into the roasting time, squeeze the juice from 2 oranges and pour over the duck. ❧ When the duck is done (test by inserting a sharp knife into the thigh, if the juices run clear the duck is well done), remove the garlic, rosemary, and orange zest from the cavity. ❧ Transfer the duck to a casserole with the cooking juices and vegetables and spoon the caramelized orange zest over the top. Place over a moderate heat for 5 minutes, turning the duck once or twice. ❧ Serve hot.

# Scottiglia
## *Mixed Meat Stew*

*Serves 6*
*Preparation: 25 minutes*
*Cooking: 1¼ hours*
*Recipe grading: fairly easy*

- 5 tablespoons extra-virgin olive oil
- 2 cloves garlic, finely chopped
- 1 medium onion, finely chopped
- 1 small carrot, finely chopped
- 1 small stalk celery, finely chopped
- 1½ tablespoons finely chopped parsley
- 1 tablespoon finely chopped fresh basil
- 2 crumbled dried chili peppers
- about 2¾ lb/1.3 kg assorted meat, game, and poultry (veal, pork, rabbit, guinea fowl), trimmed and cut into small pieces
- ½ cup/4 fl oz/125 ml full-bodied, dry red wine
- 3 tablespoons tomato purée
- salt to taste
- freshly ground black pepper
- 4¼ cups/1¾ pints/1 liter hot stock (homemade or bouillon cube)
- 6 fairly thin slices of firm-textured, white or brown bread, 2 days old
- 1 clove garlic, whole

*Suggested wine: a dry red*
*(Chianti dei Colli Fiorentini)*

Pour the oil into a heavy-bottomed saucepan and sauté the garlic, onion, carrot, celery, parsley, basil, and chili peppers. ☙ After 5 minutes, add the meat, game, and poultry and cook for 8 minutes over a slightly higher heat. ☙ Pour in the wine, increase the heat, and cook, uncovered, for about 7 minutes to reduce the liquid. ☙ Add the tomato purée, season with salt and pepper, and stir well. ☙ Pour in the stock. Lower the heat, cover and simmer for about 1 hour, stirring occasionally. There should be plenty of liquid when the dish is cooked; it should be halfway between a hearty soup and a casserole. ☙ Cut each slice of bread in half and toast. Rub the toast with the whole clove of garlic, place in heated soup bowls, and ladle in the stew. ☙ Leave to stand for 2–3 minutes before serving so that the bread can absorb some of the liquid.

# Francesina

## *Boiled Beef with Onions*

If you have to cook the beef first, put it in a large saucepan with cold water to cover. Add the onion, carrot, celery, parsley, tomatoes, and sea salt and bring slowly to a boil. Simmer gently for about 1 hour until the beef is very tender. Leave to cool in the cooking liquid to make it easier to cut when cold. ⊷ Sauté the sliced onions in the oil in a large heavy-bottomed saucepan over a moderate heat for 2–3 minutes. ⊷ Add half the stock, partially cover and cook for 10 minutes, or until reduced. ⊷ Chop the meat into small pieces or thin slices. ⊷ Add the meat to the onions, season with salt and pepper, and stir for 3–4 minutes. ⊷ Stir in the tomatoes, cover and simmer over a low heat for about 15 minutes. If necessary, moisten with some of the remaining stock. ⊷ Serve hot.

*Serves 4*

*Preparation: 15 minutes*

*Cooking 30 minutes + 1 hour for boiling the beef*

*Recipe grading: easy*

- 1½ lb/750 g leftover boiled beef (brisket, rump roast or bottom round/brisket, topside or silverside)
- 1 onion, cut in half
- 1 carrot, cut in 3–4 pieces
- 1 stalk celery, cut in 3–4 pieces
- sprig of parsley
- 4 ripe tomatoes, pricked with a fork
- 1 tablespoon coarse sea salt
- 3 large onions, very thinly sliced
- 4 tablespoons extra-virgin olive oil
- 1 cup/8 fl oz/250 ml beef stock (homemade or bouillon cube)
- salt to taste
- freshly ground black pepper
- 1¾ cups/14 oz/400 g canned Italian tomatoes, sieved

*Suggested wine: a dry red (Chianti Classico)*

*This dish is a delicious way of using up the beef from Bollito Misto (Mixed Boiled Meats), which is usually cooked in large quantities. If you are cooking the meat especially for this dish, it is best if cooked the day before. Francesina is equally good reheated.*

# Cacciucco

*Mixed Fish Stew*

To make the fish stock, pour the water into a large, deep saucepan and add the onion, carrot, celery, parsley, and bay leaf. Cover and bring to a boil. ❧ Add the hake and sea robin. When back on the boil reduce the heat, cover and simmer for 20 minutes. ❧ Strain the stock into a large bowl. Push the flesh of the fish through a sieve or flake finely and add to the bowl with the stock. ❧ Heat the oil in a large, heavy-bottomed saucepan and sauté the chopped onion, garlic, parsley and chili peppers for 5 minutes. ❧ Chop the octopus in pieces about 1 in/2.5 cm square. Separate the tentacles from the body of the cuttlefish (if not already done). Cut the squids' body sacs in half. ❧ Add the octopus, cuttlefish, and squid to the pan and cook for 5 minutes. ❧ Pour in the wine and reduce over a slightly higher heat. ❧ Stir in the tomatoes and season with salt and pepper. Cover and simmer for 20 minutes. ❧ Add the fish stock, dogfish or shark, and shrimp. Cover and cook for 10 minutes, stirring gently at intervals. ❧ Toast the bread and rub the slices all over with the whole clove of garlic. ❧ Place a slice in each soup bowl, ladle the seafood stew over the top, and leave to stand briefly before serving.

*Serves 6*
*Preparation: 50 minutes*
*Cooking: 11/4 hours*
*Recipe grading: fairly easy*

- 4¼ cups/1¾ pints/1 liter salted water
- 1 onion, cut in half
- 1 carrot, cut lengthwise in half
- 1 stalk celery, cut in half
- small bunch of parsley
- 1 bay leaf
- 8 oz/250 g filleted hake
- 8 oz/250 g sea robin/gurnard, cleaned
- 4 tablespoons extra-virgin olive oil
- ½ onion, finely chopped
- 4 garlic cloves, finely chopped
- 3 tablespoons finely chopped parsley
- 2 crumbled dried chili peppers
- 8 oz/250 g each of baby octopus, small cuttlefish, and small squid (ask your fish vendor to prepare by removing the stomach, bony parts and the ink sacs)
- 1 cup/8 fl oz/250 ml dry white wine
- 1¾ cups/14 oz/400 g canned tomatoes, drained and diced
- salt to taste
- freshly ground black pepper
- 8 oz/250 g smooth dogfish or shark/ smooth hound or shark, cleaned and cut in pieces
- 8 oz/250 g shrimp/prawns, heads removed but not peeled
- 4 slices firm-textured, white bread
- 1 clove garlic, whole

*Suggested wine: a dry red (Sassicaia) or a dry white (Bianco di Nugola)*

# Tuscan Wine

For centuries Tuscan wine was synonymous with Chianti, and the classic straw-wrapped flasks sprang to mind whenever the name was heard abroad. Unfortunately, the name, and the flask, also became associated with much that was lackluster (and worse) in red wines. All this has changed over the last thirty years and Tuscan winemakers are now among the most innovative in Italy. Dating from the times of the Chianti League in the 13th century, the name originally referred to the area north of Siena (the southern part of today's Chianti Classico zone), but as the wine became more popular this century it was extended south below Siena, east to Arezzo, and north and west toward Florence and

Pisa. Chianti wines are traditionally made from a combination of Sangiovese, Canaiolo, Malvasia, and Trebbiano grapes. Although Chianti is still the most widely produced wine, some of the older wines, such as *Vernaccia di San Gimignano* and *Vino Nobile di Montepulciano*, have been revived and modernized, while relative newcomers, including *Brunello di Montalcino* and table wines such as *Sassicaia*, have won awards and acclaim in Italy and internationally. Tuscany's traditional dessert wine – *Vin Santo*, or Holy Wine – is still produced, and enjoyed, while a recent trend has seen a huge increase in the number of *Vin Novellos*, very young, new season's wine, on sale from early November after harvest.

*The Castello di Brolio in the province of Siena is part of the Ricasoli family estates. In the first half of the 18th century Baron Bettino Ricasoli improved Chianti wines by laying down strict guidelines. Winemaking in Tuscany has always been linked to the regions' illustrious families. Three of the big names in Tuscan viticulture today, Ricasoli, Frescobaldi, and Antinori, date back over 600 years.*

Brunello di Montalcino *is Tuscany's most famous, and arguably Italy's best, red wine. In Tuscan terms, it is a relatively new wine, since it was first made in the 1880s by Ferruccio Biondi-Santi. Centered on the tiny town of Montalcino, the Brunello-producing region is very small and the wines themselves expensive. A Brunello has to be aged for at least five years, and many need far longer to reach their full potential. Recently, winegrowers have begun producing* Vino Rosso di Montalcino, *which can be a very good, younger alternative to Brunello. Faced with some real competition, in recent years the neighboring hilltop town of Montepulciano has greatly improved its traditional red,* Vino Nobile di Montepulciano.

*Although Tuscany is traditionally associated with red wines, some very respectable whites are grown as well.* Vernaccia di San Gimignano, *which has been grown near the medieval town of San Gimignano since at least 1286, is perhaps the best-known. Other traditional whites include* Bianco Vergine Valdichiana, Bianco di Pitigliano, Montecarlo, Bianco Pisano di San Torpè, *and wines from the island of Elba. Winemakers are now developing a host of non-traditional whites for modern palettes.*

*While the great red wines are aged in wooden and stainless steel barrels in underground cellars, Tuscany's most famous dessert wine –* Vin Santo *– is aged in casks in special lofts where it is exposed to extremes of temperature.* Vin Santo *ranges from very sweet to very dry; all are acceptable and the degree of dryness preferred is left to personal taste.* Vin Santo *is traditionally served with* Biscottini di Prato *(see recipe, page 108). Other Tuscan dessert wines, now almost unobtainable, include sweet red* Aleatico *and golden* Moscato *from the island of Elba, and* Moscadelletto *of Montalcino.*

# Fagioli con Salsicce
*Italian Sausages and Beans*

*Serves 4*

*Preparation: 5 minutes + 12 hours
soaking if dried beans are used*

*Cooking: 35 minutes + time to cook the
beans*

*Recipe grading: easy*

- 8 medium Italian pork sausages
- ½ cup/4 fl oz/125 ml hot water
- 5 tablespoons extra-virgin olive oil
- 2 cloves garlic, finely chopped
- 4 fresh sage leaves
- 2 cups/1 lb/500 g canned Italian
  tomatoes, sieved
- salt to taste
- freshly ground black pepper
- 1½ lb/750 g fresh cannellini beans,
  precooked, or 2 cups/12 oz/350 g dried
  cannellini beans, soaked and precooked

*Suggested wine: a dry red
(Chianti dei Colli Fiorentini)*

*This traditional Florentine dish makes
a hearty meal in itself. If short of time,
use two cans of high quality
Cannellini (or white kidney beans or
great northern) beans.*

Pierce the sausages in 3 or 4 places and put into a nonstick skillet. Add the hot water and cook over a fairly high heat for about 10–12 minutes, turning frequently. ❧ Pour the oil into a large, nonstick skillet and add the garlic. Cook over a low heat with the sage, tomatoes, and salt and pepper for 5 minutes. ❧ Increase the heat and cook for 10 minutes. Add the beans and sausages, cover and cook over a moderate heat for 15 minutes, stirring occasionally. ❧ Serve very hot.

# Seppie in Zimino

## *Cuttlefish Casserole*

Chop the cuttlefish into small pieces. ❧ Wash the spinach very thoroughly and boil in a little salted water for about 10 minutes. Drain well, squeeze out the excess moisture and chop coarsely. ❧ Pour the oil into a large, heavy-bottomed saucepan and sauté the onion, garlic, carrot, celery, parsley, and chili peppers for 4–5 minutes. ❧ Stir in the cuttlefish. Season with salt and pepper and pour in the wine. Cook, uncovered, for 5–6 minutes to reduce. ❧ Add the spinach and cook for 3–4 minutes before adding the tomatoes. Taste and add more salt if necessary, mix well, cover and leave to simmer for 30 minutes, stirring occasionally. ❧ Serve hot.

*Serves 4*
*Preparation: 25 minutes*
*Cooking: 1 hour*
*Recipe grading: fairly easy*

- 2 lb/1 kg small cuttlefish (ask your fish vendor to prepare these by removing the stomachs and bony parts)
- 2 lb/1 kg fresh spinach
- 5 tablespoons extra-virgin olive oil
- 1 onion, finely chopped
- 2 cloves garlic, finely chopped
- 1 small carrot, finely chopped
- 1 small stalk celery, finely chopped
- 1½ tablespoons parsley, finely chopped
- 2 crumbled dried chili peppers
- ½ cup/4 fl oz/125 ml dry white wine
- salt to taste
- freshly ground black pepper
- 1¾ cups/14 oz/400 g canned Italian tomatoes, chopped

*Suggested wine: a dry white (Vernaccia di San Gimignano)*

*If you can't get cuttlefish, use small tender squid in its place. In this case make sure that your fish vendor also removes the ink sacs.*

# Trippa alla Fiorentina

## *Tripe Florentine-Style*

*Serves 4*
*Preparation: 20 minutes*
*Cooking: 45 minutes*
*Recipe grading: easy*

Rinse the tripe thoroughly under cold running water, drain and dry with a clean cloth. Cut into thin strips with kitchen scissors or a very sharp knife. ✂ Sauté the onion, carrot, and celery in the oil in a heavy-bottomed flameproof casserole for 5 minutes. ✂ Add the tripe and season with salt and pepper. Continue cooking for 3–4 minutes, stirring continuously. ✂ Add the wine and cook over a higher heat, uncovered, for 5–6 minutes to reduce. ✂ Mix in the tomatoes and check the seasoning. Cover and leave to simmer for 30 minutes, stirring occasionally. If necessary, reduce the amount of liquid by cooking, uncovered, over a higher heat for a few minutes. ✂ Serve very hot with the cheese served separately.

- 2 lb/1 kg ready-to-cook calf's honeycomb tripe
- 1 large onion, finely chopped
- 1 large carrot, finely chopped
- 1 stalk celery, finely chopped
- 4 tablespoons extra-virgin olive oil
- salt to taste
- freshly ground black pepper
- ½ cup/4 fl oz/125 ml dry white wine
- 1¾ cups/14 oz/400 g canned Italian tomatoes, sieved
- scant 1 cup/3½ oz/100 g freshly grated parmesan cheese

*Suggested wine: a dry red (Pomino)*

*Mobile tripe vendors still sell many types of tripe sandwiches or plastic containers full of delicious tripe on Florentine street corners.*

# Agnello al Forno
## *Tuscan Roast Lamb*

*Serves 6*

*Preparation time: 10 minutes +
    2 hours' marinating*

*Cooking time: 1 hour*

*Recipe grading: easy*

- 2 lb/1 kg leg or shoulder of lamb
- 3 cloves garlic, each sliced into three
- 1 tablespoon chopped fresh rosemary
- ½ cup/4 fl oz/125 ml white wine vinegar
- salt to taste
- freshly ground black pepper
- ½ cup/4 fl oz/125 ml extra-virgin olive oil

*Suggested wine: a dry red
    (Brunello di Montalcino)*

Using a small, pointed knife, make deep slits in the meat and push a slice of garlic and some rosemary into each incision. ๛ Mix the vinegar with the salt, pepper, remaining rosemary, and oil in a large deep bowl and add the meat. ๛ Leave to stand for 2 hours, turning the meat several times in the marinade. ๛ Preheat the oven to 200°C/400°F/gas 6. Place the meat in a roasting pan, pour the marinade over the top, and roast for about 1 hour (depending on whether the lamb is to be pale pink in the center or well done), basting at intervals. ๛ Serve with roast potatoes.

# Spezzatino Toscano

*Serves 4*

*Preparation: 20 minutes*

*Cooking: 1¼ hours for veal, 1¾–2 hours for beef*

*Recipe grading: easy*

- 2 lb/1 kg shank or shoulder/ shin or shoulder of veal, or beef chuck, round or shank/beef chuck or shin
- ½ cup/2 oz/60 g all-purpose/plain flour
- 2 cloves garlic, finely chopped
- 1 tablespoon finely chopped fresh sage
- 1 tablespoon finely chopped fresh rosemary
- 4 tablespoons extra-virgin olive oil
- 4 canned Italian tomatoes, drained
- salt to taste
- freshly ground black pepper
- 1 cup/8 fl oz/250 ml dry red wine
- ½ cup/4 fl oz/125 ml stock (homemade or bouillon cube)

*Suggested wine: a dry red (Chianti Rufina)*

*Country-style potatoes make a delicious accompaniment to this classic Tuscan casserole. To prepare: sauté a finely sliced onion in a little olive oil, then add 1 can of drained, chopped tomatoes and 1 lb/500 g of boiled or steamed potatoes cut into fairly small pieces. Stir over a moderate heat for 5 minutes before serving.*

# Spezzatino Toscano
## *Classic Tuscan Casserole*

Trim the meat and cut into 1 in/2.5 cm cubes. Lightly coat all over with flour, shaking off the excess. ॐ In a heavy-bottomed saucepan, sauté the garlic, sage, and rosemary in the oil for 3–4 minutes. ॐ Add the meat and brown the pieces all over for 5–6 minutes. ॐ Add the tomatoes, salt, and pepper and cook for another 5 minutes. ॐ Pour in the wine, cover and simmer for 1 hour (longer for beef) until tender. If necessary add some of the stock to keep moist. Taste and add more salt if desired. ॐ Serve hot.

# Fegato alla Salvia

## *Calf's Liver with Sage*

Serves 4
Preparation: 5 minutes
Cooking: 10 minutes
Recipe grading: easy

Lightly flour the liver, shaking off any excess. ❧ Heat the oil with the garlic and sage over a moderate heat in a large nonstick skillet. When the oil starts to sizzle around the garlic, raise the heat to moderately high. Add the liver and cook quickly to ensure tenderness, turning once. ❧ Sprinkle with a little salt and pepper when well-browned and remove from the heat. ❧ Serve at once with puréed potatoes, or boiled or steamed spinach, briefly sautéed in garlic-flavored oil.

- 1¼ lb/625 g calf's liver, thinly sliced
- ½ cup/2 oz/60 g all-purpose/plain flour
- 4 tablespoons extra-virgin olive oil
- 3 cloves garlic
- 6 fresh sage leaves
- salt to taste
- freshly ground black pepper

*Suggested wine: a young dry red
(Rosso di Montepulciano)*

*This simple, elegant dish, also known as* Fegato alla Fiorentina *(Sautéed Calf's Liver, Florentine-Style), originally comes from the Tuscan capital, although it is becoming more and more difficult to find in the city's trattorias and restaurants.*

# Cooking in Renaissance Florence

The Renaissance is synonymous with the rebirth of the arts and the revival of Classical Greek and Roman ideas and values. It is also synonymous with the Tuscan capital city of Florence, where it began and where so many of its greatest artists lived and worked. Under the guidance of the Medici family, Florence became a major center of European cultural and intellectual life and remained so for over three hundred years. Among the arts fostered by the Medici, cooking and "the art of entertaining" occupied an important place. The Medici and other noble Florentine families held sumptuous banquets where guests feasted on staggering quantities of extravagant foods. One such dinner, on the occasion of the marriage (by proxy!) of Marie de' Medici with Henri IV of France, took place in the Palazzo Vecchio on October 5, 1600. Giambologna and Piero Tacca created the most expensively ephemeral statues in history, made of sugar: the cost of the raw material alone amounted to some 1,700 gold florins. Emilio de' Cavalieri's music accompanied the whole banquet which was served in five "services" or "removes": the first was a cold buffet with 24 different courses, including wild boar molds and jellies with live fish encased in them. The second, known as a "kitchen" service, comprised 9 courses of hot dishes, among them pies which the pastrycooks had decorated with the family crest; this was followed by two more hot "services" of 18 and 10 courses respectively, including game and various meat dishes. The banquet ended with a final "service" of fruit, cheeses, and desserts.

Meat and game were usually the main dishes served at banquets. The meat was generally cooked with a variety of spices and with fruit. The fruit helped to mask the taste of meat that quickly went bad because it could not be kept cold, while spices, so rare and difficult to come by, were proof of the host's wealth and power.

Many of the Medici court artists were connisseurs of fine cooking: the letters of Bronzino, Pontormo, Andrea del Sarto, and Cellini contain many references to suppers and banquets, listing dishes they had particularly enjoyed: artichoke frittatas, eggs and asparagus, roast lamb, and pea soup are among the many mentioned by name.

With the assistance of artists such as Bernardo Buontalenti, the Medici family's banquets evolved into what can truly be described as a "theater of marvels," famed for mechanical devices which caused entire banqueting tables to vanish, only to be replaced by others, ready laid and decorated for the next stage of the banquet. Buontalenti also used "ghiacciaie" or underground stores of ice (and from which a street in Florence, Via delle Ghiacciaie, takes its name) to ensure that even in the hottest summer weather his master, Francis I, could indulge his love of drinks made with crushed ice, an early form of flavored water-ices.

Another member of the Medici family – Catherine de' Medici – left her native Florence for France when she was only fourteen years old, with her recipe books and her retinue of cooks, to marry Henry de Valois, the future King of France. Catherine introduced the French to many Tuscan delicacies, including duck with sweet oranges, crespelle (crêpes), an early form of béchamel made with olive oil, the art of frying, and the use of olive oil, spinach, peas, and artichokes.

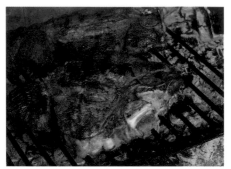

# Bistecca alla Fiorentina
*Florentine Beef Steak*

*Serves 2*
*Preparation: 1 minute*
*Cooking: about 10 minutes*
*Recipe grading: easy*

- a 1½ lb/ 750 g T-bone steak from a young steer, at least 1½ in/4 cm thick
- salt to taste
- freshly ground black pepper

*Suggested wine: a dry red*
  *(Brunello di Montalcino)*

Season the steak well with pepper. ❧ Place on a grill about 4 in/10 cm above the glowing embers of a wood fire. ❧ After 4–5 minutes the steak will come away easily from the grill. Sprinkle the seared surface with a little salt, turn and cook the other side, sprinkling again with salt and a little more pepper. ❧ When cooked, the steak should be well-browned and sealed on the outside, rare and juicy inside. ❧ Serve at once.

*A grilled Florentine T-bone steak is the ultimate treat for steak-lovers. In Italy the steak is cut from Tuscan-bred Chianina beef and hung for at least 6 days. Traditionally it is cooked over the embers of a charcoal or wood-burning grill and eaten very rare. The steaks are also very good barbecued. Ask your butcher for a steak which has been well-hung to ensure plenty of flavor and tenderness.*

# Pollo ai Semi di Finocchio

## *Chicken with Fennel Seeds*

Wash the chicken inside and out and dry with paper towels. ❧ Mix the pancetta, garlic, herbs, and fennel seeds with a good pinch each of salt and pepper and place in the cavity. Use a trussing needle and thread to sew up the opening. ❧ Pour half the olive oil into a roasting pan and add the chicken. Drizzle with the remaining oil, and sprinkle with pepper and salt. ❧ Roast for 1 hour or until the juices run clear when a knife is inserted deep into the thigh. ❧ Serve hot, accompanied by a mixed green salad.

*Serves 4*
*Preparation: 20 minutes*
*Cooking: 1 hour*
*Recipe grading: easy*

- a young, oven-ready roasting chicken, about 3½ lb/1.5 kg
- scant ½ cup/3½ oz/100 g finely chopped pancetta
- 2 cloves garlic, finely chopped
- 1 heaped teaspoon finely chopped fresh sage
- 1 heaped teaspoon finely chopped fresh rosemary
- 1 tablespoon finely chopped parsley
- 1 level teaspoon fennel seeds
- 5 tablespoons extra-virgin olive oil
- salt to taste
- freshly ground black pepper

*Suggested wine: a young dry red (Chianti Putto)*

# Frittata di Bietole

## *Swiss Chard Frittata*

*Serves 4*
*Preparation: 5 minutes*
*Cooking: 20 minutes*
*Recipe grading: fairly easy*

Bring a little salted water to a boil and cook the Swiss chard over a moderate heat for about 10 minutes. Drain well, squeeze out excess moisture, and chop coarsely. ⚥ Break the eggs into a bowl. Beat briefly with a fork and season with salt and pepper. Stir in the cheese, followed by the prosciutto and cooked Swiss chard. ⚥ Heat the oil in a fairly large nonstick skillet over a moderate heat and when it is hot, pour in the egg mixture and cook for about 5 minutes, until the eggs have set and the underside is lightly browned. ⚥ To turn the frittata, place a large plate over it, turn both upside down and then slide the egg mixture back into the pan, browned side up. Cook for 3–4 minutes more. ⚥ Turn the cooked frittata out onto a heated serving dish. ⚥ Serve at once with green or red chicory/Belgian endive or radicchio.

- 1 lb/500 g trimmed tender young Swiss chard, well-washed
- 6 large fresh eggs
- salt to taste
- freshly ground black pepper
- ½ cup/2 oz/60 g freshly grated parmesan cheese
- ¼ cup/2 oz/60 g finely chopped prosciutto
- 4 tablespoons extra-virgin olive oil

*Suggested wine: a young, dry rosé (Bolgheri)*

*Replace the Swiss chard with the same amount of spinach to make an equally delicious frittata.*

# Verdure

Like all traditional cuisines, until recently Tuscan vegetable cooking was strongly linked to the seasons and the vegetables each one produced. Spring was the season for fava beans and pecorino cheese, summer was a vegetable-lovers paradise when zucchini, peppers, eggplants, tomatoes, green beans, peas, and many others vied with each other for a place on the table. Fall and winter brought artichokes, fennel bulbs, and dried beans to the fore. All this has changed in the last ten years since most vegetables have become available at affordable prices throughout the year.

# Fagiolini alla Fiorentina

## *Florentine String Beans*

Cook the beans in boiling, salted water until they are tender but still crisp. Drain and set aside. ✌ Heat the oil in a skillet over a moderate heat and sauté the garlic and onion or shallot for 3–4 minutes. ✌ Add the fennel seeds, tomatoes, and salt to taste and simmer for 3–4 minutes before adding the cooked beans. ✌ Season with pepper and mix carefully. Cover and cook for about 12 minutes. If the mixture dries out too much during cooking, moisten with the water. ✌ Serve hot.

*Serves 4*
*Preparation: 15 minutes*
*Cooking: 35 minutes*
*Recipe grading: easy*

- 1¼ lb/625 g string/French beans, washed, topped, and tailed
- 4 tablespoons extra-virgin olive oil
- 1 clove garlic, finely chopped
- 1 onion or shallot, very thinly sliced
- 1 teaspoon crushed fennel seeds
- 2 large ripe tomatoes, skinned, seeded and diced
- salt to taste
- freshly ground black pepper
- 1–2 tablespoons hot water

*Wine: a light, dry white (Bianco Pisano di San Thorpé)*

# Stufato di Fave

## *Fava Bean Stew*

*Serves 4*

*Preparation: 15 minutes*

*Cooking: 25 minutes*

*Recipe grading: easy*

- 4 cups/1 lb/500 g freshly hulled fava beans/broad beans (about 5 lb/2.5 kg of fresh bean pods)
- scant ½ cup/3½ oz/100 g finely chopped pancetta
- 2 cloves garlic, bruised
- 1 onion, thinly sliced
- 4 tablespoons extra-virgin olive oil
- 1½ tablespoons finely chopped parsley
- salt to taste
- freshly ground black pepper
- 1 cup/8 fl oz/250 ml hot chicken or vegetable stock (homemade or bouillon cube)

*Suggested wine: a dry white (Vernaccia di San Gimignano)*

Put the beans in a bowl and cover with cold water to prevent their skins from toughening. ❧ Sauté the pancetta, garlic, and onion in the oil in a large skillet for 5–6 minutes over a moderate heat. ❧ Remove the garlic and add the drained beans, parsley, salt, pepper, and stock. Cover and simmer over a moderate heat for about 20 minutes, or until the beans are very tender. ❧ Reduce any remaining stock by increasing the heat with the lid removed. ❧ Serve hot.

*This stew is equally good when made with frozen beans.*

# Fiori di Zucca Fritti

## *Fried Zucchini Flowers*

*Serves 4*
*Preparation 10 minutes*
*Cooking: 25 minutes*
*Recipe grading: fairly easy*

Remove the pistil (the bright yellow center) and calyx (the green leaflets at the base) from each flower. Wash quickly and gently pat dry with paper towels. ❧ Sift the flour into a mixing bowl, make a well in the center, and add the salt and 1 tablespoon each of oil and water. ❧ Gradually mix into the flour, adding enough extra water to make a batter with a thick pouring consistency that will cling to the flowers. ❧ Heat the oil in a large skillet until very hot. ❧ Dip 4–6 flowers in the batter and fry until golden brown on both sides. Drain on paper towels. Fry all the flowers in the same way. ❧ Serve immediately.

- 14 oz/400 g very fresh zucchini/courgette flowers
- scant 1 cup/3½ oz/100 g all-purpose/plain flour
- ½ teaspoon salt
- 1 tablespoon + scant 1 cup/7 fl oz/200 ml extra-virgin olive oil
- 1–2 tablespoons cold water

*Wine: a dry white (Elba Bianco)*

*Replace the water with the same quantity of beer. The batter will be much crisper, with its own special taste.*

*Serves 4*

*Preparation: 15 minutes + 10–15 minutes' standing*

*Cooking: 30 minutes*

*Recipe grading: fairly easy*

- 8 very young globe artichokes
- juice of 1 lemon
- 1 clove garlic, finely chopped
- 1½ tablespoons finely chopped parsley
- scant ½ cup/3½ oz/100 g finely chopped pancetta
- 1 cup/2 oz/60 g fine fresh breadcrumbs
- 6 tablespoons extra-virgin olive oil
- salt to taste
- freshly ground black pepper

*Suggested wine: a dry white (Montecarlo Bianco)*

# Carciofi Ripieni

*Stuffed Artichokes*

Prepare the artichokes by cutting off the tops and removing the tough outer leaves. Cut the stalk at the base so that they will stand upright on their own. Peel the stems and place them in a bowl of cold water with the artichokes and lemon juice. Set aside for 10–15 minutes. ❧ Chop the stems finely and place in a bowl with the garlic, parsley, pancetta, and breadcrumbs. Add 2 tablespoons of oil and mix well. ❧ Drain the artichokes and pat dry with paper towels. ❧ Open each artichoke and push a little of the breadcrumb mixture firmly down to the base of each leaf. ❧ Pack the stuffed artichokes upright in a flameproof pan only just large enough for them. Add the remaining oil and enough water to come halfway up the artichokes. ❧ Bring to a gentle boil, cover tightly and simmer for 25–30 minutes. Test by removing one of the lowest, outermost leaves; if it is tender, they are done. ❧ Continue cooking, uncovered, over a high heat until all the cooking liquid has evaporated. ❧ Serve hot, warm or cold.

# Fagioli in Fiasco

## *Beans Cooked in a Flask*

Feed the beans into the flask. Pour in the oil, add the garlic, sage, tomatoes, salt and pepper, then top up with the water. ❧ Cork up the flask tightly and place the bulbous end deep among the barely glowing embers of a wood fire to cook gently for several hours. These flasks used to be left in the embers last thing at night. By the morning the beans were cooked. ❧ Tip the beans out of the flask. Discard the garlic and sage and serve, with an extra drizzle of olive oil, salt, and freshly ground black pepper.

*Serves 4*
*Preparation: 10 minutes*
*Cooking: at least 3 hours*
*Recipe grading: easy*

- 1½ lb/750 g freshly hulled cannellini beans or 2 cups/12 oz/350 g dried cannellini beans, soaked for 12 hours
- ½ cup/4 fl oz/125 ml extra-virgin olive oil
- 2 cloves garlic, whole
- 4 fresh sage leaves
- 2 cherry tomatoes, skins pricked with a fork
- salt to taste
- freshly ground black pepper
- water, sufficient to fill the flask to three-quarters

*Suggested wine: a young, dry red*
*(Chianti dei Colli Fiorentini)*

*This is a traditional Florentine recipe which may appeal to the adventurous cook as an enjoyable experiment. You will need an empty, straw-wrapped Tuscan wine bottle and its cork. Remove the straw, leaving a glass flask. In the modern version of this recipe the beans are cooked in a special earthenware container like the one shown here. If you do try this recipe, be sure to place the bottle in the dying embers and not in the flames. If you put it in the flames, it may well explode.*

# Feast Days: Keeping Tradition Alive

Like most people, Tuscans can usually think of a good reason to throw a party. Rural feast days, known as *sagre,* often have very old, pagan origins and are usually held to give thanks for nature's bounty. Christian festivals, such as those held to celebrate the town or village Patron Saint's Day, occur alongside celebrations to commemorate important political or local events.

Each of these events is associated with an array of typical dishes.

In Tuscany Christmas is popularly known as *ceppo,* the equivalent of the English "Yuletide", a shared reference to the custom of burning a large log of wood, the Yule Log, on Christmas Eve while work started in the kitchen to prepare the capon for the main meal next day.

*The Palio, held twice a year in June and August, is the most famous celebration in Siena. But Christmas is a special time too, with an abundance of seasonal specialties, from the legendary* Panforte, *made from a centuries-old recipe with candied fruits, almonds, honey, sugar and spice (see recipe, page 114), to* Cavallucci *(see recipe, page 117), made with honey, sugar, flour, candied fruits, and pepper, so-called because they were given to the stable boys (called "cavallari" in Italian) employed in country inns, and* Riccarelli *(see recipe, page 116), another very old recipe for cookies made with almonds and sugar.*

For Berlingaccio (Fat Thursday, the last before Lent), synonymous with over-indulgence and to be repented of the following Ash Wednesday, it was customary to slaughter the fattened pig which would not only replenish the family larder with various cuts of meat but also provide excellent fare for the feast day: blood puddings and pork fat used to prepare Schiacciata alla Fiorentina and Cenci (see recipe, page 112), the traditional Florentine cakes and cookies of Carnevale.

At New Year and Epiphany in Viareggio little witch-shaped cookies are made with flour, eggs, sugar, anise, milk, and rhum. The sweet dough is rolled out into a thin sheet and stamped out with special pastry cutters to represent a seasonal vistor from popular folklore, a kindly old witch (the Befana).

Throughout the year, but particularly in the summer months, the villages and hilltop towns of Tuscany celebrate historical events and customs with parades, medieval flag-throwing, archery or jousting competitions, as well as a host of food and wine festivals and events. The magic of walking into a medival village such as San Quirico d'Orcia on a hot summer's night to find the whole village feasting at a long table stretching down the main street is unforgettable.

Easter in Florence is celebrated every year with the Scoppio del Carro (Explosion of the Carriage) on Easter Sunday in Piazza Duomo. A good explosion bodes well for the fall harvest.

Serves 4

*Preparation: 30 minutes + time to make the meat sauce*

*Cooking: 45 minutes*

*Recipe grading: fairly easy*

- 1 quantity meat sauce (see recipes, page 45, 50 or 53 )
- 2 whole, tender celery bunches with plenty of heart, washed
- 5 oz/150 g chicken livers
- 2 tablespoons/1 oz/30 g butter
- 2 tablespoons + scant 1 cup/7 fl oz/ 200 ml extra-virgin olive oil
- 1 onion, finely chopped
- 1 clove garlic, finely chopped
- generous ½ cup/5 oz/150 g finely chopped prosciutto
- 1¾ cups/7 oz/200 g ground lean veal
- ½ cup/4 fl oz/125ml dry white wine
- ½ cup/2 oz/60 g all-purpose/plain flour
- 2 eggs, beaten
- 1 cup/3 oz/90 g dry breadcrumbs
- salt to taste
- freshly ground black pepper
- 1 cup/4 oz/125 g freshly grated parmesan cheese

*Suggested wine: a dry, fruity red (Chianti Montalbano)*

# Sedani alla Pratese
## *Stuffed Celery Stalks*

Prepare the meat sauce. ❧ Boil the celery in a large pan of salted water for 5 minutes. Drain and cool. ❧ Trim any connective tissue and discolored parts from the chicken livers and chop finely. ❧ Heat the butter with the 2 tablespoons of oil in a nonstick skillet. When foaming, add the onion and garlic and sauté for 3–4 minutes. ❧ Add the chicken livers and prosciutto and cook for a few minutes, then add the veal, breaking up any lumps. ❧ Season with salt and pepper, stir and cook for 4–5 minutes. ❧ Pour in the wine, cover and cook over a low heat for 20 minutes. ❧ Cut the celery stalks into 3 in/7.5 cm lengths and pack each one with the chicken liver stuffing. ❧ Coat each piece of celery with flour, dip in the egg and coat with breadcrumbs. ❧ Heat the remaining oil in a large nonstick skillet and fry 3–4 of the stalks until golden brown on both sides. Drain on paper towels. Repeat until all the stalks are fried. ❧ Place a layer of celery stalks in a warm ovenproof dish. Spoon some meat sauce and any remaining stuffing over the top and sprinkle with a little cheese. Repeat until all the celery, meat sauce, and cheese are used up. Be sure to finish with a layer of cheese. ❧ Bake in a preheated oven at 425°C/220°C/gas 7 until the cheese turns golden brown. ❧ Serve at once.

*Serves 4*

*Preparation: 10 minutes + 10–15 minutes' standing*

*Cooking: 15 minutes*

*Recipe grading: fairly easy*

- 8 baby globe artichokes, or 16 frozen artichoke hearts, defrosted
- juice of 1 lemon
- 1/2 cup/2 oz/60 g all-purpose/plain flour
- 1/2 cup/4 fl oz/125 ml extra-virgin olive oil
- 5 large fresh eggs
- salt to taste
- freshly ground black pepper

# Tortino di Carciofi
### *Italian Artichoke Omelet*

If using fresh artichokes, cut off the tops and remove the tough outer leaves. Cut the stalk at the base leaving 3/4 in/2 cm of the stem attached. Wash, cut into quarters and place in a bowl of cold water with the lemon juice for 10–15 minutes (this will stop them turning black). ⁊ Drain well and pat dry. ⁊ Coat the artichoke pieces or defrosted hearts with flour, shaking off any excess. ⁊ Heat all but 2 tablespoons of the oil in a large, nonstick skillet over a high heat until very hot. ⁊ Fry the artichokes for about 8 minutes, turning them several times so that they cook evenly. When they are lightly browned, drain on paper towels. ⁊ Tip out the oil used for frying and replace with the remaining oil. Arrange the artichokes in the skillet and return to a moderately high heat. ⁊ Beat the eggs lightly with the salt and pepper then pour over the artichokes. Cook for 4–5 minutes. ⁊ Turn the omelet carefully and cook for 4 minutes more. It should be firm and lightly browned on both sides. ⁊ Turn out onto a heated serving dish and serve hot.

*Suggested wine:*
*a young, dry white*
*(Bianco Vergine Valdichiana)*

**Use frozen artichoke hearts unless you can find tiny, very fresh artichoke buds.**

# Piselli alla Montaperti

## *Peas with Pancetta, Garlic, and Wine*

*Serves 4*

*Preparation 10 minutes + time for hulling/shelling the peas*

*Cooking: 25 minutes*

*Recipe grading: easy*

Rinse the peas in a colander under cold water. ❧ Sauté the onion or shallot, garlic, parsley, and pancetta together in the oil over a moderate heat for 2 minutes. ❧ Add the peas, season with salt and pepper, and stir well. ❧ Pour in the wine, cover and simmer gently for 15–20 minutes, stirring occasionally. Moisten with a little stock as necessary. ❧ Serve hot.

- 4 cups/1¼ lb/625 g hulled fresh peas or frozen petits pois
- 1 small white onion or shallot, very thinly sliced
- 1 clove garlic, finely chopped
- 1½ tablespoons finely chopped parsley
- ½ cup/4 oz/125 g diced pancetta
- 4 tablespoons extra-virgin olive oil
- salt to taste
- freshly ground black pepper
- ½ cup/4 fl oz/125 ml dry white wine
- scant ½ cup/3½ fl oz/100 ml stock (homemade or bouillon cube)

*Suggested wine: a young, dry, lightly sparkling red (Vino Novello)*

# Funghi Trifolati

## *Mushroom Stew*

*Serves 4*
*Preparation: 10 minutes*
*Cooking: 30 minutes*
*Recipe grading: easy*

Trim the ends off the mushroom stalks. Brush away any dirt and grit and wash quickly under cold running water. Pat dry with paper towels. ✤ Slice the caps into thin strips and dice the stalks. ✤ Sauté the garlic in the oil with the calamint over a low heat for 3–4 minutes. When the garlic starts to color, add the mushroom stalks. Season with salt and pepper and cook for 5 minutes. ✤ Add the caps and cook for another 5 minutes. If necessary, stir in enough hot water to keep the mushrooms moist. ✤ Finally, stir in the tomato pureé, and more seasoning, if needed. ✤ Simmer gently for 10–12 minutes. ✤ Serve hot.

- 2 lb/1 kg fresh porcini mushrooms
- 3 cloves garlic, whole
- 4 tablespoons extra-virgin olive oil
- sprig of fresh calamint (or parsley or thyme)
- salt to taste
- freshly ground black pepper
- 1–2 tablespoons hot water
- scant 1 cup/7 fl oz/200 ml tomato purée

*Suggested wine: a dry white*
  *(Vernaccia di San Gimignano)*

*This same recipe can be made with a variety of wild mushrooms. Cooking times may vary according to the type of mushroom used. For a stronger mushroom flavor, omit the tomato purée. These mushrooms make a delicious side dish and a wonderful sauce for fresh pasta.*

# Cipolle alla Grossetana
## *Stuffed Onions*

*Serves 4*

*Preparation: 25 minutes*

*Cooking: 1 hour*

*Recipe grading: fairly easy*

- 8 large Bermuda or yellow onions/mild red or Spanish onions
- 1 oz/25 g dried porcini mushrooms, soaked in about ½ cup/4 fl oz/125 ml warm water
- 2 tablespoons extra-virgin olive oil
- 1 cup/4 oz/125 g ground lean veal
- 1 fresh Italian pork sausage
- 1 egg
- 1 tablespoon finely chopped parsley
- salt to taste
- freshly ground black pepper
- freshly grated nutmeg
- 2 tablespoons/1 oz/30 g butter
- 6 tablespoons stock (homemade or bouillon cube)

*Suggested wine: a young, dry red (Chianti Classico)*

Cut both ends off the onions. Put into a saucepan and cover with salted boiling water. Cook over a fairly high heat for 10 minutes. Drain. ❧ Carefully push the center out of each onion, leaving the 2–3 outermost layers intact to be stuffed. Set aside. ❧ Finely chop the center sections. ❧ Drain the mushrooms well, pour the liquid through a fine sieve and reserve. ❧ Chop the mushrooms finely and sauté in the oil in a small skillet for 3 minutes. ❧ Add the veal and sausage meat, using a fork to crush any lumps that may form. Cook for 10 minutes, moistening with the reserved mushroom liquid as necessary. ❧ Combine the chopped onion, egg, parsley, salt, pepper, and nutmeg in a large bowl with the meat mixture. Mix well and stuff the onions. ❧ Arrange the onions in a large, shallow ovenproof dish greased with the butter and pour half the stock over the top. ❧ Bake in a preheated oven at 400°F/200°C/gas 6 for 30 minutes, adding more stock at intervals, if necesssary. ❧ Serve hot.

# Dolci

In keeping with the rest of Tuscan cooking and with the Tuscan temperament itself, traditional desserts are simple and closely linked to natural products produced in the region: honey, hazelnuts, almonds, raisins, grapes, rosemary, and chestnuts are typical ingredients. Essential simplicity and style might be the best way to sum up a Tuscan dessert. Try finishing a four-course meal with a glass of *Vin Santo* and a handful of Prato cookies for dunking and ponderous munching.

# Zuccotto

## *Ice Cream Trifle*

Cut the cake in half horizontally, then divide it into 8–12 triangular wedges. ❧ Moisten the cake on both sides with Cointreau or rum and use to line a 3½ pint/2¾ pint/1½ litre capacity mold. ❧ Beat the cream until stiff, adding the sugar when almost ready. Fold in the grated chocolate, almonds, and candied fruits. ❧ Transfer half this mixture to a separate bowl. ❧ Melt the remaining chocolate in a double boiler (or in a bowl over boiling water) and mix gently into one half of the cream. ❧ Spread the white cream over the sponge cake lining in the mold. Cover with foil and place in the freezer for 10–15 minutes. ❧ Remove the foil and spoon the chocolate cream into the mold, which should be completely full. ❧ Cover with foil and freeze for at least 3–4 hours before serving.

*Serves 4*

*Preparation: 15 minutes + 3–4 hours' freezing*

*Cooking: 10 minutes*

*Recipe grading: fairly easy*

- 12 oz/375 g good quality, store-bought fatless sponge cake (Madeira type)
- ½ cup/4 fl oz/125 ml Cointreau or rum
- 2 cups/16 fl oz/500 ml light whipping cream
- ½ cup/2 oz/60 g confectioners'/icing sugar
- 2 squares/2 oz/60 g good quality semi-sweet/unsweetened dark chocolate, grated
- 3 tablespoons/1 oz/30 g peeled, finely chopped almonds
- ¼ cup/2 oz/60 g diced candied orange and citron peel
- 2½ squares/2½ oz/75 g semi-sweet/unsweetened dark chocolate e.g. Meonier, coarsely chopped

*Suggested wine: a dry, sparkling white (Vernaccia di San Gimignano spumante)*

# Frittelle di Riso

## *Lemon Rice Fritters*

Cook the rice in the milk for about 1 hour or until the grains have almost disintegrated. ❧ Stir the butter into this very thick mixture and remove from the heat. ❧ Add the sugar and the rind. Stir in the eggs one at a time, then add the salt, flour, raisins, and rum. Stir thoroughly and chill for about 1 hour in the refrigerator. ❧ Heat the oil in a nonstick skillet until very hot. To test, drop a tiny piece of fritter into the oil. If bubbles form around it immediately, it is hot enough. ❧ Scoop the fritter mixture up in tablespoonful-size lots and place in the hot oil. Fry 5–6 fritters together until they are golden brown all over. This should take about 4 minutes for each batch. ❧ Drain on paper towels. Dust with sugar and transfer to a heated serving dish. ❧ Serve at once.

*Serves 4–6*

*Preparation: 20 minutes +1 hour chilling*

*Cooking: 1¼ hours*

*Recipe grading: fairly easy*

- 1 cup/7 oz/200 g short-grain, pudding rice (or sticky rice)
- 2 cups/16 fl oz/500 ml whole/full cream milk
- 1 tablespoon/½ oz/15 g butter
- 3 tablespoons granulated/caster sugar
- grated rind of ½ lemon or orange
- 2 eggs
- dash of salt
- ½ cup/2 oz/60 g all-purpose/plain flour
- ⅓ cup/2 oz/60 g raisins/sultanas, soaked in warm water for 15 minutes, drained and squeezed
- 3½ tablespoons rum
- scant 1 cup/7 fl oz/200 ml olive oil for frying
- scant 1 cup/3½ oz/100 g confectioners'/icing sugar

*Suggested wine: a medium or dry dessert wine (Vin Santo)*

*These scrumptious fritters originally come from Siena where they were served on Saint Joseph's day (March 19).*

# Schiacciata con l'Uva
## *Black Grape Sweet Bread*

*Serves 6*

*Preparation: 25 minutes + 3 hours'
rising*

*Cooking: 30 minutes*

*Recipe grading: fairly easy*

- 1 tablespoon/$^1$/$_2$ oz/15 g fresh
  compressed/baker's yeast or 1$^1$/$_2$ packets
  active dried yeast
- scant $^1$/$_2$ cup/3$^1$/$_2$ fl oz/100 ml lukewarm
  water
- 2$^1$/$_4$ cups/8 oz/250 g unbleached or all-
  purpose flour/strong or plain flour
- $^1$/$_2$ teaspoon salt
- scant $^1$/$_2$ cup/3$^1$/$_2$ fl oz/100 ml extra-virgin
  olive oil
- $^2$/$_3$ cup/5 oz/150 g superfine/caster sugar
- $^1$/$_2$ cup/2 oz/60 g all-purpose/plain flour
- 2 lb/1 kg unpeeled ripe, black grapes,
  seeded

*Suggested wine: a slightly sweet, sparkling
white (Moscadello di Montalcino)*

Dissolve the yeast in the water and set aside for about 15 minutes. ✥ Sift the flour and salt into a large mixing bowl and make a well in the center. Add the frothy yeast liquid and gradually combine with the flour. ✥ Transfer to a floured work surface and knead briefly. ✥ Shape the dough into a ball, wrap loosely in a clean cloth, and leave to rise for 1 hour in a warm place. ✥ Knead again, gradually working in three-quarters of the oil, one-third of the sugar, and a little more salt. ✥ Shape into a ball, wrap in a cloth, and leave to rise for another hour. ✥ Use the remaining oil to grease a rectangular 11 x 16 in/28 x 40 cm baking pan. ✥ Divide the dough in half and press one half into the pan ✥ Gently press just over half the grapes into the dough and sprinkle with half the remaining sugar. Roll the rest of the dough out into a rectangular shape and use it to cover the grapes. ✥ Press the remaining grapes into this top layer and sprinkle with the remaining sugar. ✥ Leave to stand at warm room temperature for 1 hour to rise, then bake in a preheated oven at 375°F/190°C/gas 5 for 30 minutes. ✥ Serve warm or cold.

*This delicious black grape sweet bread appears
in bakeries and cake shops from August as the
new season's grapes mature.*

# Pan di Ramerino
*Rosemary Bread Rolls*

*Yields 6 rosemary bread rolls*

*Preparation 25 minutes + 1¹/₂ hours rising*

*Cooking: 25 minutes*

*Recipe grading: easy*

- 1 tablespoon/¹/₂ oz/15 g fresh compressed/baker's yeast or 1¹/₂ packets active dried yeast
- ²/₃ cup/5 fl oz/150 ml lukewarm water
- small branch of fresh rosemary, washed and dried
- 4 tablespoons extra-virgin olive oil
- 3 cups/12 oz/350 g unbleached white/strong white flour + ¹/₂ cup/ 2 oz/60 g extra flour
- ¹/₄ cup/2 oz/60 g superfine/caster sugar
- 1 teaspoon salt
- ¹/₂ cup/3¹/₂ oz/100 g Muscatel dried grapes (seeded) or seedless white raisins/golden sultanas, washed
- 1 egg, lightly beaten

*Suggested wine: a slightly sweet, sparkling white (Moscadello di Montalcino)*

*These sweet bread rolls are an old Florentine recipe. They were traditionally served at Easter. Bakers set up stalls outside church doors, selling the rolls to churchgoers on their way home. It was sacrilege to waste even the tiniest crumb!*

Dissolve the yeast in the water and leave to stand for 15 minutes. ☙ Strip the leaves off the rosemary, reserving the smaller, younger ones. ☙ Place the larger leaves and the oil in a small saucepan over a low heat for about 5 minutes. ☙ Strain the oil through a fine sieve into a small bowl, discarding the rosemary. ☙ Sift the flour into a large mixing bowl, make a well in the center and add the frothy yeast liquid. Gradually incorporate the flour, sugar, rosemary-flavored oil, and salt. ☙ Transfer the dough to a floured work surface and knead well. ☙ Shape into a ball and place in a large bowl. Cover with a clean cloth and leave to rise for 1 hour. ☙ Work the raisins into the risen dough, together with the reserved rosemary, kneading to distibute them evenly. ☙ Divide the dough into 6 equal balls and flatten slightly. ☙ Space out on a nonstick baking sheet. Brush with egg, mark with a cross, and leave to rise again for 30 minutes. ☙ Bake in a preheated oven at 400°F/200°C/gas 6 for 20 minutes.

# Castagnaccio
## *Chestnut Batter Pudding*

Sift the flour into a mixing bowl and make a well in the center. Pour in the water, 1 tablespoon of the oil, and salt. Stir thoroughly to obtain a thick, lumpfree, pouring batter. ❧ Stir in the drained raisins and the nuts and then pour into a baking pan greased with 2 tablespoons of the oil. ❧ Sprinkle with the rosemary leaves and drizzle with the remaining oil. ❧ Bake in a preheated oven at 400°F/200°C/gas 6 for about 30 minutes, or until a thin crunchy crust has formed. ❧ Serve hot or at room temperature.

*Serves 4*
*Preparation: 15 minutes*
*Cooking: 30 minutes*
*Recipe grading: fairly easy*

- 2¾ cups/10 oz/300 g sweet chestnut flour
- 1½ cups/12 fl oz/375 ml water
- 6 tablespoons extra-virgin olive oil
- dash of salt
- ½ cup/3 oz/90 g small seedless white raisins/small, golden sultanas, soaked in warm water for 15 minutes, drained and squeezed
- ⅓ cup/2 oz/60 g pine nuts
- a few young, tender rosemary leaves

*Suggested wine: a dry dessert wine*
  *(Vin Santo)*

*Use a larger pan if you prefer your castagnaccio thinner and more crunchy, or smaller if you like a creamier, softer texture under the crust.*

# Biscottini di Prato

## *Prato Cookies*

*Serves 6*

*Preparation: 15 minutes*

*Cooking: about 40 minutes*

*Recipe grading: easy*

- scant 2 cups/8 oz/250 g sweet almonds, unpeeled
- 4 egg yolks
- 2 cups/1 lb/500 g sugar
- 4 cups/1 lb/500 g all-purpose/plain flour
- dash of salt
- 1 tablespoon butter
- ¼ cup/1 oz/30 g all-purpose/plain flour

*Suggested wine: a sweet, medium or dry dessert wine (Vin Santo)*

Spread the almonds out in a shallow baking pan and roast at 400°F/200°C /gas 6 for 4–5 minutes. ❧ When cool enough to handle, skin and chop finely. ❧ Beat the egg yolks and sugar together in a mixing bowl until pale and fluffy. ❧ Stir in the flour, almonds, and salt gradually, using a fork and then combining by hand. ❧ Knead the mixture quickly but thoroughly on a floured work surface. ❧ Shape the dough into long cylinders about ½ in/ 1 cm in diameter. ❧ Transfer to a buttered and floured cookie sheet. Bake in a preheated oven at 375°F/190°C/gas 5 for 25 minutes. ❧ Remove from the oven and raise the temperature to 400°F/200°C/gas 6. ❧ Slice the cylinders diagonally into pieces 1½ in/4 cm long, and return them to the oven for 10 minutes more, or until pale golden brown.

*Be sure to roast the almonds. The cookies will lack their distinctive flavor and texture if unroasted ground almonds are used. Served with a glass of Vin Santo (Holy wine) for dipping.*

# Brutti ma Buoni

## *Almond Cookies*

Use a deep bowl and electric beater to beat the egg whites until stiff but not "dry". ❧ Fold in the ground almonds and sugar. ❧ Transfer to a large bowl over a pan of simmering water. Cover and cook for 20 minutes. ❧ Use a tablespoon to scoop out egg-shaped spoonfuls and place them on a lightly buttered and floured cookie sheet. ❧ Bake in a preheated oven at 350°F/180°C/gas 4 for about 45 minutes or until they are golden brown. ❧ Leave to cool before serving.

*Serves 6*
*Preparation: 15 minutes*
*Cooking: 1¼ hours*
*Recipe grading: easy*

- 6 egg whites
- 7 cups, loosely packed/1¼ lb/625 g ground almonds
- 2 cups/1 lb/500 g granulated or superfine/caster sugar
- 1 tablespoon/½ oz/15 g butter
- ¼ cup/1 oz/30 g all-purpose/plain flour

*Suggested wine: a sweet, medium or dry dessert wine (Vin Santo)*

*These can be served in their own with a sweet dessert wine such as Vin Santo or together with the Prato Cookies.*

# Ongoing Tradition

While it is commonplace nowadays to find a Milanese risotto or a southern dish of pasta with broccoli on the menu of a restaurant in Tuscany, nevertheless Tuscan cooking retains a precise identity with distinctive flavors and aromas linked to the region's culinary traditions and to its famous olive oil. Furthermore, Tuscan cooking has recently rediscovered dishes steeped in tradition, made with their original ingredients: spelt (or emmer wheat), a cereal widely used by the Etruscans, is once more appreciated with the reintroduction of spelt soup, alongside such innovations as spelt or barley salads with fresh vegetables. Traditional Tuscan cooking has always been typified by the use of absolutely fresh produce. Plenty of filling soups and nutritious "minestre," very little pasta, and beans in preference to rice, provide a diet that is low in fat, modest and digestible, based on ingredients which can easily be used up as leftovers, avoiding any waste. See, for example, *Panzanella* (see recipe, page 29), *Pappa al Pomodoro* (see recipe, page 32), or *Francesina* (see recipe, page 63). The few desserts are good, plain fare: *Castagnaccio* (see recipe, page 107) or *Schiacciata all'Uva* (see recipe, page 104), with one exception: *Zuppa Ducale* or "the Duke's trifle" created by Siennese cooks in honor of the Duke of Correggio (see recipe, next page).

## ZUPPA INGLESE

Serves eight to ten people. If you can't get the special Alchermes liqueur, double the quantity of rum and add 1 teaspoon of red food coloring.

5 egg yolks

²/₃ cup/5 oz/150 g sugar

¹/₃ cup/1¹/₂ oz/45 g all-purpose/plain flour

2 cups/16 fl oz/500 ml milk

few drops of vanilla extract/essence

3¹/₂ squares/3¹/₂ oz/100 g grated semi-sweet/unsweetened dark chocolate

¹/₂ cup/4 fl oz/125 ml Alchermes liqueur

¹/₂ cup/4 fl oz/125 ml rum

4 tablespoons water

20 ladyfingers/sponge fingers (about 8 oz/250 g)

whipped cream for decoration

Whisk the egg yolks and sugar until straw-colored and then stir in the flour. ❧ Heat the milk with the vanilla extract until fairly hot, but not boiling. ❧ Pour the milk into the egg mixture and then cook for 7–8 minutes in a heavy-bottomed saucepan over a low heat, stirring continuously to prevent lumps forming. ❧ Pour half the custard into a bowl and cover with plastic wrap touching the surface to prevent a skin forming. ❧ Melt the chocolate in a small pan over a larger pan of boiling water or in a double boiler. ❧ Return the remaining custard to the heat and stir in the melted chocolate. Cook for 2 minutes, stirring continuously. ❧ Pour the chocolate custard into a bowl and cover with plastic wrap touching the surface to prevent a skin forming. ❧ Set the custards aside to cool before using. ❧ Mix the Alchermes, rum, and water together in a bowl. ❧ Dip the ladyfingers into the water and liqueur mixture, then use one-third of them to line a 2-quart glass bowl or soufflé dish. ❧ Pour the chocolate custard over the top, cover with another layer of dipped ladyfingers and spread the plain custard on top. ❧ Finish with the remaining ladyfingers, cover with foil, and refrigerate for about 12 hours. ❧ Just before serving, decorate with plenty of whipped cream and, if liked, a little more grated chocolate.

*Zuppa Ducale became famous in Florence during the 18th century as "Zuppa Inglese." It was renamed by the proprietor of the historic Florentine Caffé Doney (closed long ago) to reflect its great popularity with early members of the English expatriate community which has existed in Florence for more than two centuries. In Tuscany this wickedly rich trifle, made with lashings of egg custard and chocolate, is streaked crimson by the cochineal (made with crushed Kermes-oak insects) in the reputedly highly aphrodisiac Alchermes liqueur manufactured by the monks of St. Mark's monastery.*

# **Cenci**

*Fried Carnival Cookies with Confectioners' Sugar*

*Serves 4*

*Preparation: 20 minutes + 30 minutes' standing*

*Cooking: about 20 minutes*

*Recipe grading: easy*

- 2 cups/8 oz/250 g all-purpose/plain flour + ½ cup/2 oz/60 g extra
- 2 tablespoons/1 oz/30 g butter, softened
- 2 eggs
- ¼ cup/2 oz/60 g granulated/caster sugar
- 1½ tablespoons Vin Santo or other good quality sweet dessert wine
- dash of salt
- 1½ tablespoons grated orange rind
- 1¼ cups/10 fl oz/300 ml extra-virgin olive oil for frying
- ½ cup/2 oz/60 g confectioners'/icing sugar, sifted

*Suggested wine: a sweet, medium or dry dessert wine (Vin Santo)*

Sift the flour onto a work surface and make a well in the center. Add the butter, eggs, sugar, dessert wine, salt, and orange rind. Gradually combine with the flour and knead well. The dough should be soft but hold its shape well. ❧ Cover with a clean cloth and leave to rest for 30 minutes. ❧ Roll out into a thin sheet using a lightly floured rolling pin. ❧ Cut into diamonds, rectangles, and broad rectangular strips which can be tied loosely into a knot if wished. ❧ Heat the oil to very hot and fry a few at a time until pale golden brown all over. ❧ Remove with a slotted spoon and drain on paper towels. ❧ Serve at once, sprinkled with confectioners' sugar.

*Cenci (which means "rags") are traditionally served during Carnivale, the period leading up to Lent before Easter.*

# Panforte

## *Siennese Dried Fruit and Nut Cake*

Serves 6
*Preparation: 30 minutes*
*Cooking: about 1 hour*
*Recipe grading: fairly easy*

- scant 2 cups/8 oz/250 g peeled whole almonds
- generous 1 cup/5 oz/150 g walnuts
- scant ½ cup/3½ oz/100 g small, soft dried figs
- 1¼ cups/10 oz/300 g best quality mixed candied peel (ideally orange, citron and melon), finely chopped
- 1 tablespoon ground spice mixture (cinnamon, cloves, coriander seeds, white peppercorns, and nutmeg)
- ½ cup/2 oz/60 g unsweetened cocoa powder
- 1¼ cups/5 oz/150 g confectioners'/icing sugar + extra for finishing
- scant ½ cup/3½ oz/100 g clear, runny honey
- 1½ tablespoons all-purpose/plain flour
- butter for greasing pan
- confectioners' wafer papers or rice paper for lining the pan

*Suggested wine: a sweet, medium or dry dessert wine (Vin Santo)*

Spread the almonds and walnuts out on cookie sheets and bake at 400°F/200°C/gas 6 for 3–4 minutes. Leave to cool slightly and then chop very finely (ground almonds will not give the same texture). ❧ Mix the nuts in a large bowl with the finely chopped figs (remove the hard stalk end), the peel, spices and cocoa powder. ❧ Set aside while you dissolve the sugar in the honey in the top of a double boiler or a bowl over simmering water. After about 8 minutes, test to see if it forms a thread when you lift a spoonful above the pan. If not, continue cooking for a few minutes more. ❧ Remove from the heat and stir in the flour and the nuts and figs mixture. Put into a shallow layer cake pan with a removable base which has been buttered and lined with the wafers or rice paper. Smooth the surface and cover with a layer of wafers or rice paper. ❧ Bake in a preheated oven at 350°F/180°C/gas 4 for about 40 minutes. Leave to cool, then dust with the sugar and place on a serving dish.

**Panforte will keep for months if wrapped in foil.**

# Ricciarelli
## *Marzipan Petits Fours*

Spread the almonds out on a cookie sheet and bake in a preheated oven at 400°F/200°C/gas 6 for 3–4 minutes. Then grind them in a mortar and pestle and put into a mixing bowl. ❧ Stir in the sugars, orange peel, and almond extract and carefully fold in the egg white. ❧ Shape the mixture into lozenges or squares and place on rice paper or wafers, trimming off the excess. Put on cookie sheets and leave to stand in a cool place for about 10 hours. ❧ Bake in a preheated oven at 300°F/150°C/gas 2 for about 1 hour, reducing the heat if they show signs of browning. They should remain quite soft. ❧ Remove from the oven and dust with sugar. ❧ Serve when they have cooled.

*Serves 4–6*

*Preparation: 25 minutes + 10 hours' resting for the dough*

*Cooking: 1 hour*

*Recipe grading: fairly easy*

- scant 2 cups/8 oz/250 g peeled whole almonds
- 1 cup/7 oz/200 g superfine or granulated/caster sugar
- scant 1¼ cups/5 oz/150 g confectioners'/icing sugar + extra for dusting
- scant ¼ cup/1½ oz/45 g finely chopped candied orange peel
- few drops almond extract
- 1 egg white, stiffly beaten
- confectioners' wafers or rice paper

*Suggested wine: a sweet, medium or dry dessert wine (Vin Santo)*

*Although the Ricciarelli keep well for a few days, they are at their best when freshly baked.*

# Cavallucci

## *Siennese Cookies with Spices, Honey, and Nuts*

Using a double boiler or a bowl over simmering water, heat the sugar and honey together. When a thread of honey forms when a spoonful is lifted above the bowl, remove from the heat and gently fold in the flour together with the walnuts, peel, anise, and coriander. ❧ Flour your hands to stop the mixture sticking to them and break off pieces of the dough, rolling them into small cylinders. Cut them into slices about 1 in/2.5 cm thick and form into curved shapes. ❧ Put onto a buttered and floured cookie sheet and bake in a preheated oven at 325°F/160°C/gas 3 for about 1 hour.

*Serves 6*
*Preparation: 20 minutes*
*Cooking: 1¼ hours*
*Recipe grading: fairly easy*

- 1 cup/8 oz/250 g sugar
- ⅓ cup/3½ oz/100 g clear, runny honey
- 3 cups/12 oz/350 g all-purpose/plain flour + about ¼ cup/1½ oz/45 g extra
- ½ cup/2 oz/60 g chopped walnuts
- ¼ cup/2 oz/60 g finely chopped candied orange and citron peel
- 1 teaspoon freshly ground anise seeds
- freshly ground coriander seeds
- butter for geasing the cookie sheet

*Suggested wine: a sweet, medium or dry dessert wine (Vin Santo)*

*Cavallucci will keep fresh and crisp for several days in a tightly sealed container.*

# Index

118

# Acknowledgments

The Publishers would like to thank Mastrociliegia, Fiesole (Florence)
who kindly lent props for photography..

All photos by MARCO LANZA except:

GIULIANO CAPPELLI, FLORENCE: COVER (LANDSCAPE), BACK COVER (C, CR, B), 1,
2, 3, 5, 6, 7B, 11T, 12T, 13B, 13T, 21B, 21CL, 21T, 32T, 35T, 36T, 36B, 37TL,
37TR, 48, 66T, 66B, 67T, 67TR; GIUSEPPE CARFAGNA, ROME: 90B, 91TR, 91B;
FARABOLAFOTO, MILAN: 9T, 43B, 67CL; ADRIANO NARDI, FLORENCE: 90T, 91TL,
112; NIEDERSÄCHSISCHES LANDESMUSEUM, LANDESGALERIE, HANNOVER, 76; ARCHIVIO
SCALA, FLORENCE: 8, 77R